WEST INDIAN READERS

BOOK FIVE

THE TRIAL SCENE FROM "THE MERCHANT OF VENICE." (*See page 262.*)
(*From the painting by Sir James D. Linton, P.R.I.*)

NELSON'S

WEST INDIAN READERS

Book FIVE

Compiled by J. O. Cutteridge

NELSON THORNES

First edition published in 1928 by Thomas Nelson & Sons, with subsequent revisions.

This edition published in 2013 by:
Nelson Thornes Ltd
Delta Place
27 Bath Road
CHELTENHAM
GL53 7TH
United Kingdom

13 14 15 16 17 / 10 9 8 7 6 5 4 3 2

A catalogue record for this book is available from the British Library

ISBN 978 1 4085 2356 8

Page make-up by Compuscript Ltd
Printed by Multivista Global Ltd

Acknowledgements

The author and the publisher would also like to thank the following for permission to reproduce material:

Text Permissions

P48–9: reprinted by permission of The Society of Authors as the Literary Representative of the Estate of John Masefield.

Images

pII: 'In which predicament, I say thou standst', illustration from 'The Merchant of Venice', c.1910 (colour litho), Linton, Sir James Dromgole (1840–1916)/Private Collection/The Bridgeman Art Library; p19: J.R. Skelton; p33: In Camera Stock/Alamy; p34: Lawrie Williams/Getty Images; p35: Susan E Degginger/Alamy; p37: Sir John Everett Millais, P.R.A; p43: India Picture/Alamy; p46: Ugo Ambroggio/Alamy; p73: The Fighting Temeraire, 1839 (oil on canvas), Turner, Joseph Mallord William (1775–1851)/National Gallery, London, UK/The Bridgeman Art Library; p87: Blickwinkel/Alamy; p110: Joan of Arc (1412–31) at the Coronation of King Charles VII (1403–61) 17th July 1429, 1854 (oil on canvas), Ingres, Jean Auguste Dominique (1780–1867)/Louvre, Paris, France/Giraudon/The Bridgeman Art Library; p127: The Wood Sawyers, 1848 (oil on canvas), Millet, Jean-Francois (1814–75)/Victoria & Albert Museum, London, UK/The Stapleton Collection/The Bridgeman Art Library; p135: Robert Harding Picture Library/Alamy; p139: Art Archive/ Garrick Club; p143: Art Archive/Tate Gallery/Eileen Tweedy; p145: Art Archive/DeA Picture Library; p161: John Warburton-Lee/Alamy; p164: The Surrender of Breda, 1625, c.1635 (oil on canvas) (see also 68345), Velazquez, Diego Rodriguez de Silva y (1599–1660)/Prado, Madrid, Spain/Giraudon/The Bridgeman Art Library; p169: Rosalind in the Forest, c.1868 (oil on board), Millais, Sir John Everett (1829–96)/© Walker Art Gallery, National Museums Liverpool/ The Bridgeman Art Library; p179: George Lord Rodney (engraving), English School, (19th century)/Private Collection/ © Look and Learn/The Bridgeman Art Library; p199: View of Salisbury Cathedral from the Bishop's Grounds, (oil on canvas) c.1822, Constable, John (1776–1837)/Victoria & Albert Museum, London, UK/The Bridgeman Art Library; p217: Prince Arthur and Prince Hubert, 1882 (oil on canvas), Yeames, William Frederick (1835–1918)/Manchester Art Gallery, UK/The Bridgeman Art Library; p219: Inga Spence/Alamy; p220: Fotos Van Robin/Getty Images; p221: Anne Bolt; p227: Author's Image Ltd/Alamy; p236: Chardin; p241: Hoekkuk; p246–247: Mr. W. Scott, B.Sc; p249: Deddeda Design Pictures/Corbis; p251: Hywit Dimyadi/Alamy; p269: Detail of Madonna and Child with saints and angels (oil on panel), Bellini, Giovanni (c.1430–1516)/Gallerie dell'Accademia, Venice, Italy/Cameraphoto Arte Venezia/The Bridgeman Art Library; p288: Art Archive/Tate Gallery/Eileen Tweedy.

Every effort has been made to trace the copyright holders but if any have been inadvertently overlooked the publisher will be pleased to make the necessary arrangements at the first opportunity.

PREFATORY NOTE FOR TEACHERS

THIS book completes the series of six books (Introductory, and Books I. to V.) of West Indian Readers. These books should meet the needs of the average West Indian school, but if still more advanced material is required for town schools where larger numbers of pupils stay to complete the sixth and seventh standards, teachers should provide a wide range of books in the school library for the purpose. "The proper business of those who are ready for the senior stage is not learning to read, but reading" (English Board's "Suggestions," 1927). The books from which the literary extracts in this series have been taken, and which have been named in the Prefatory Note in each book, will form an admirable library for the purpose. Books of travel, or descriptions of other countries, should now be frequently read, and those in the "World Revealed" Series, published by Thomas Nelson and Sons in their "Teaching of English" Series.

Teachers are reminded that the exercises at the ends of the lessons are given as *types*. They should compile others on similar lines, and add further examples to those given.

The historical lessons of Books III. and IV. have been continued in this book to complete the outline of the story of the West Indies.

The literature given in this book should be supplemented by the following books:

1. *Gulliver's Travels*. Nelson's "Told to the Children" Series.
2. *Gulliver's Voyage to Lilliput*. Nelson's "Graded Readings."
3. *Crusoe and Gulliver*. Nelson's "Teaching of English" Series.
4. *Great Expectations*. Nelson's "Dickens for Boys and Girls."
5. *Fabre's Book of Insects*. Nelson's "Teaching of English" Series.
6. *Ivanhoe*. Nelson's "Historical Romances" Series or Nelson's Classics.

7. *The Approach to Shakespeare.* Nelson's "Teaching of English" Series.

8. *Little Plays from Shakespeare.* First and Second Series. Nelson's "Teaching of English" Series.

9. *The Merchant of Venice.* Nelson's "Teaching of English" Series.

10. *As You Like It.* Nelson's "Teaching of English" Series.

11. *Diamond Rock.* Nelson's "Stories for Boys."

As in previous books, assistance has been rendered by Dr. J. R. Dickson, Mr. R. O. Williams, and Mr. T. Spencer, to whom my thanks are due, as well as to Sir Francis Watts, K.C.M.G., who has again kindly read the proofs and offered valuable suggestions and criticisms. The lessons on "Insect Pests" follow closely the substance of the pamphlet *Insect Pests of the Lesser Antilles* (Ballou), published by the Imperial Department of Agriculture, and I acknowledge with gratitude the permission granted by the Principal of the Imperial College of Tropical Agriculture to utilize the matter and illustrations therefrom. Many of the interesting facts in the Readers have been culled from the various books of Sir Algernon Aspinall, C.M.G., C.B.E., with his permission, and to him also I am greatly indebted for the interest he has taken in this work. The illustrations of sugar machinery have been kindly supplied by Messrs. Duncan Stewart, Ltd., Glasgow, the well-known manufacturers of sugar factory appliances, and the diagram of the layout of the factory has been prepared by Mr. W. Scott, B.Sc., Professor of Sugar Technology, Imperial College of Tropical Agriculture.

Inspectors and teachers are reminded that suggestions for modifications of future editions, local names and references, etc., will be gratefully received. In conclusion, though conscious of their many shortcomings, I trust the books have done much to supply the long-felt want of Readers specially prepared for the schools of the West Indies, from the West Indian point of view, and that the interest of the pupils has been awakened in consequence.

J. O. CUTTERIDGE.

CONTENTS

An Asterisk (*) indicates Poetry.

LESSON 1

COTTON

DURING the last century there was a tremendous development in cotton manufactures. Besides its use as material for a great variety of common articles, cotton has now taken the place of wool in many fabrics, and in recent years it has almost entirely supplanted linen as a material for clothing. It is treated with caustic soda to give it many of the properties of silk, and is commonly used as "artificial silk" in place of the more costly natural material. The great improvement in the wearing qualities of motor-car tyres is also due to the use of cotton in their manufacture, and cotton fibre is the basis of very powerful explosives.

This increased demand for the raw material of cotton has caused its cultivation to become one of the most important agricultural pursuits in the tropics. The industry is a flourishing one in the West Indies in the islands of Antigua, Barbados, Grenada, Montserrat, Nevis, St. Lucia, St. Kitts, and St. Vincent, and we should thus learn something about it.

Cotton cultivation was practised in the West Indies and in Central and South America long before the New World was made known to the Old. Columbus found the plant growing abundantly when he landed here in 1492. It was one of the staple crops of the early colonists, and soon became an article of export. Even in the year 1800 the amount sent to Europe was 25,000 bales. For a time,

Cotton Flower.

owing to the development of the sugar trade and the rise of the cotton-growing industry in the United States, there was a steady decline in the production of West Indian cotton. With the world's increased demand it has since recovered, and is again one of our most important industries.

The cotton plant belongs botanically to the order of the mallows, or *Malvaceæ,* and is closely related to the ochroes, hollyhocks, and hibiscus of our gardens. Most of the species are shrubs or small plants. Cotton plants have large yellow, white, or red flowers, which are followed by pods, capsules, or "bolls." When these are ripe they burst, revealing the white cotton fibres attached to the seeds. You can see a seed with its fibres in the picture on next page.

Ripe Boll.

There are two principal varieties of cotton, long-staple cotton and short-staple cotton. The best-known of the latter is American Upland cotton, which is a kind in very great demand. It was originally a native of Mexico, but is now cultivated in the United States and in other parts of the world. Each seed bears both long and short hairs, the latter remaining attached to the seed after the long ones are removed, so that the seeds present a fuzzy appearance. The fibre or staple is usually about one inch in length. A somewhat similar kind is grown in India.

The variety chiefly grown in the West Indies is a long-staple cotton, and is known as Sea Island cotton. This is the most valuable kind of all owing to the great length (about two inches) of its fibre and its silky character. These qualities enable the spinners to use it for special purposes for which the short-fibred cottons are unsuitable. The seeds bear long hairs only, and are left quite clean when these are pulled off.

Seed with Fibres.

Sea Island cotton is often thought to be a native of the West Indies, but the probability is that it was produced by crossing other varieties, and was introduced into the "Sea Islands" off the coast of Carolina, whence it derives its name. The bulk of the world's production of this particular kind now comes from St. Vincent, Montserrat, and the other Leeward Islands. The Egyptian type of cotton is also classed as a long-staple cotton.

Cotton is distinctly a warm climate plant, and one that is well adapted to the conditions existing in most of the

West Indian Islands. It thrives best in a good loose soil such as a sandy loam, not exposed to strong winds, and in a district where the rainfall is neither too heavy nor too light. The plant will not do well on land with poor drainage.

The planting season varies with the islands, but is arranged so as to give dry weather during the period in which the cotton is to be picked. In sowing, only the best type of seed specially selected from the previous year's crop on a good estate should be used. This keeps up the desired characteristics of the Sea Island strain, without which our valuable type of cotton would soon degenerate. In the West Indies the cultivation of cotton is chiefly done by means of ploughs, forks, and hoes. The cotton fields should be lined out in rows four to five feet apart, and holes made in the rows at a distance of from twelve to thirty inches. The space depends on the fertility of the soil, more being necessary on rich lands.

Seeds are sown about one inch deep and about six seeds to the hole. With favourable weather the plantlets will commence to appear above the ground in four days. When they are about a fortnight old, the weaker plants should be pulled out, leaving the two strongest to develop in each hole. A fortnight later the weaker of the two should also be pulled out, leaving the stronger to grow alone. Subsequent care of the plant consists of moulding or earthing up the young plants and keeping the fields free from weeds by means of the hoe. Weeding operations should cease as soon as the cotton bolls begin to open, in order to keep the seed cotton free from dust. A sharp look-out must be kept for insect enemies, of which the plant has many, as we shall learn in a later lesson, and every means must be used to check and destroy these pests.

The cotton tree flowers in about eight weeks after sowing. The blooms develop into pods in four to six weeks, and these take from four to five months to mature and burst. As soon as the bolls are fully open the harvesting begins, the seed cotton being picked off the trees chiefly by women and children. They collect it in canvas bags, which are emptied into a sheet or a basket at the end of the rows. It is then carried to the storehouses, where it is thoroughly cleaned and sunned or dried.

The fibre has then to be separated from the seeds in the ginnery by a machine called a "gin," this name being simply a shortened form of the word engine. The process consists of passing the seed-cotton through toothed rollers, which allow the fibres to pass whilst the seed remains behind. The fibre or lint can then be packed in bales ready for export to the factories of Lancashire in England, while the seeds are used to produce oil, manure, and a valuable food for cattle which is known as oil-cake.

EXERCISES

1. Give a list of the uses mentioned in the lesson to which cotton fibre can be put.
2. Is the oil referred to in this lesson a mineral or a vegetable oil? What other oils of this class do you know?
3. What is the difference between "long-staple" and "short-staple" cotton? Name the cottons which belong to each class.
4. What steps are taken by the planters in the West Indies to produce a very high grade of Sea Island cotton? Name as many precautions as you can.

5. In many parts of the West Indies there may be seen a grand but strange-looking tree with huge buttresses at its base. It is known as the "Silk-Cotton Tree." In what ways is it like the cotton plant described in this lesson? How does it differ from the true cotton plant?

6. Fill in the blanks in the following passages:

   (a) Cotton is now established as a useful industry in ——, ——, ——, ——, and ——, while in St. —— it ranks as the chief crop.

   (b) When the plants are in ——, the appearance of the cotton —— is exceedingly ——.

   (c) The pickers —— the boll firmly with the left hand and remove the seed and cotton with the ——.

   (d) The seed is separated from the —— in the ——. The —— is then packed in bales for ——.

   (e) It is an ill wind that blows nobody any ——, and the shortage of cotton which the factories in —— suffered from in 1901 gave the West —— their ——. The planters imported cotton —— from the United ——, and soon grew the —— successfully.

LESSON 2

THE LAST BUCCANEER

Oh England is a pleasant place for them that's rich and high,
But England is a cruel place for such poor folks as I;
And such a port for mariners I ne'er shall see again,
As the pleasant Isle of Avès, beside the Spanish Main.

There were forty craft in Avès that were both swift and stout,
All furnished well with small arms and cannons round about;
And a thousand men in Avès made laws so fair and free
To choose their valiant captains and obey them loyally.

Thence we sailed against the Spaniard with his hoards of plate
    and gold,
Which he wrung with cruel tortures from Indian folk of old;
Likewise the merchant captains, with hearts as hard as stone,
Who flog men and keel-haul them, and starve them to the bone.

Oh the palms grew high in Avès, and fruits that shone like gold,
And the colibris* and parrots they were gorgeous to behold;
And the negro maids to Avès from bondage fast did flee,
To welcome gallant sailors, a-sweeping in from sea.

Oh sweet it was in Avès to hear the landward breeze,
A-swing with good tobacco in a net between the trees,
With a negro lass to fan you, while you listened to the roar
Of the breakers on the reef outside, that never touched the shore.

But Scripture saith, an ending to all fine things must be;
So the King's ships sailed on Avès, and quite put down were we.
All day we fought like bulldogs, but they burst the booms at
    night,
And I fled in a piragua,† sore wounded, from the fight.

Nine days I floated starving, and a negro lass beside,
Till for all I tried to cheer her, the poor young thing she died;
But as I lay a-gasping, a Bristol sail came by,
And brought me home to England here, to beg until I die.

And now I'm old and going—I'm sure I can't tell where;
One comfort is, this world's so hard, I can't be worse off there;
If I might but be a sea-dove, I'd fly across the main,
To the pleasant Isle of Avès, to look at it once again.

CHARLES KINGSLEY.

* Humming-birds.
† A canoe made from a hollow tree-trunk.

EXERCISES

1. Never mind for the moment whether buccaneering was good or bad. The question is whether the poet has got right into the skin of the man who is speaking, and has forgotten for the time being that he is a clergyman. What do you think?
2. Which phrase makes a kind of framework to the poem?
3. Granting that buccaneering was wrong, can you find anything good to say about this particular buccaneer?
4. The man (or the poet) has a gift for making word-pictures. Which of those in the poem do you think the best?
5. "Isle of Avès" means "Bird Island". Find it on page 6 of your West Indian Atlas*. From which island does it lie to the west?
6. Which did the buccaneer prefer—England or Avès? Why?

* *Publication may no longer be in use.*

LESSON 3

THE DESTRUCTION OF PORT ROYAL

THE latter half of the seventeenth century saw Jamaica become a British possession, and the headquarters of the pirates or buccaneers who infested the seas in those days. These lawless characters brought much wealth into the island and squandered their ill-gotten gains in its taverns. It was really to them, however, that Britain owed the rise to prosperity of her largest West Indian colony.

Even after their activities were limited by a treaty made between England and Spain, wealth continued to pour into Port Royal, then the capital of the island. The town stood at the end of the long spit of land called the Palisadoes, which forms a natural breakwater for the present Kingston harbour. All the riches of the Spanish Main flowed through the streets and busy marts of Port Royal, and the world's shipping crowded her harbour. But her days of prosperity were numbered; a doom swift and terrible was rushing upon her.

June 7, 1692, dawned with a cloudless sky. As day advanced a scorching sun ate up the morning breeze; not a breath stirred the drooping leaves; with open beaks and wings outspread birds sought the shade; animals panted and men gasped and sweltered in the stagnant heat. Towards midday a tremor scarce perceptible, a gentle shudder, ran over the earth; then followed another shudder more marked than the first, and far in the distance rose and fell a faint moaning, ever waxing in volume, ever drawing nearer and yet nearer, coming from the sea, the sky, the distant mountains—no man could say from where—a hollow moaning and rumbling that swiftly became a soul-devouring terror, and with awful crash came the destruction of Port Royal.

"Screams of anguish, cries of horror, were as quickly drowned by the rush of waters."[*] Earth opened swallowing men and buildings; wharves laden with merchandise sank out of sight; the sea breached and poured over the fortifications, overwhelming multitudes of people, tearing from their graves the buried dead. Giant billows rolled over the harbour, snapping their cables and driving to destruction vessels lying there at anchor; a frigate was dashed over the tops of submerged houses and left stranded but uninjured on dry land—land that heaved under her and rose and fell almost as did the waters from which she had been cast.

[*] Bridges, *Annals of Jamaica.*

The face of the earth rent asunder, gaped wide, and engulfed to the neck in its relentless maw[*] terror-stricken men; then closed, crushing to death the despairing wretches, leaving oftentimes a limb or a head exposed. A few persons, less unfortunate, were snatched from the grip of the land by the advancing sea, and all did not perish.

On a tombstone at a place not far distant from Port Royal, underneath the motto "*Dieu sur tout*", is this inscription: "Here lies the body of Lewis Galdy, Esquire, who departed this life at Port Royal the 22nd December 1736, aged 80 years. He was born at Montpelier in France, but left that country for his religion and came to settle in this island; where he was swallowed up in the great earthquake in 1692; and, by the Providence of God, was by another shock thrown into the sea and miraculously saved by swimming, until a boat took him up. He lived many years after in great reputation, beloved by all who knew him, and much lamented at his death."

For days after the first shock of earthquake the harbour was covered with floating dead, a hideous menace to the health and lives of the survivors. As far distant as Kingston, where then stood but a few rude huts, an evil smell from the sea poisoned the air everywhere; from every crack in the earth, from every fissure in the rocks, issued sulphurous fumes, For weeks no breeze relieved the laden atmosphere; in a cloudless sky each day blazed the cruel sun, and clouds of mosquitoes added unbearable torment to the sufferings of a despairing people.

[*] Stomach.

THE DESTRUCTION OF PORT ROYAL.

Day after day for three weeks the earthquake bellowed and rumbled and shook the entire island; there was scarce a mountain that did not change its outline. The very landscape turned from the vivid green of the rainy season in the tropics to the sombre colour of the dry season. "Thus vanished," says Mr. Bridges, "the glory of the most flourishing emporium of the New World." Vanished with it, too, nearly all the valuable official papers and public records of the island.

So perished Port Royal; it is said that on a clear day its ruins are visible in calm weather, where they lie buried deep beneath the waters. In 1859 a diver went down and succeeded in identifying the remains of old Fort James under the buoy marked "Church Buoy."

Despite the severity of this blow, Fate did not grow weary in her buffetings of this unfortunate town. With ant-like energy the settlers had set to work to rebuild their city, to repair their own shattered fortunes. Port Royal once again for a space raised her head, shipping once more crowded her harbour. But in 1703, in the midst of her crowded warehouses, a disastrous fire broke out, and ere it ceased to rage not a building remained save only the forts and the magazines.

Port Royal continued for a time to be little but a heap of ashes, still, however, the favourite haunt of the buccaneers, who yet brought wealth to the island equal almost in amount to that of the days of Morgan.

Once again from its ashes sprang another Port Royal— once again to be partially overwhelmed! In the year 1722 a tremendous hurricane devastated the ill-fated town, ships were sunk, lives were lost, irreparable damage was done to property.

Finally, in 1744, came a combination of earthquake and hurricane, the awful voice of the one blending in appalling tumult with the mighty roar of the other; and whilst men, calling to the mountains for shelter fled to the rocks for a refuge, their hearts failing them for fear, the city was levelled with the sands. Fortunately the greater part of the British West Indian fleet was then at sea, but eight ships which remained in the harbour were driven ashore, five of them being totally lost. At the same time and place no fewer than ninety-six merchant vessels sank or were driven ashore.

.   .   .   .   .

From that time dated the rapid growth of Kingston, the present capital of Jamaica. It came into existence after the destruction of Port Royal in 1692, and its importance quickly increased until, in 1872, it was made the capital instead of Spanish Town, the old St. Jago de la Vega of the Spaniards, twelve miles away to the west. By a curious coincidence it almost met with the fate of its predecessor, as on January 14, 1907, it was practically devastated by fire and earthquake. Thus by an irony of fate Kingston, which owed its existence to an earthquake, was to a great extent destroyed by a similar visitation.

EXERCISES

1. Enumerate the blows which Port Royal received at the hands of Nature. Which was the most severe blow, and which could be said to be the "knock-out" blow?
2. How long did Lewis Galdy live after the earthquake of 1692? Give your answer in years, months, and days. Of what nationality was he?

3. How can you account for the fact that 215 years later Kingston practically met with a similar fate? (See Book III., Lesson 22.)

4. Give the opposite for each of the following:

predecessor	breached
cloudless	advancing
squandered	hideous
natural	valuable
perceptible	partially

5. In what way did the resting-place of the stranded frigate resemble the sea from which it had come?

6. Give your own impressions of any earthquake shock you have experienced.

7. Make sentences of your own containing these phrases:

forming a natural break-water	a menace to the health
ever waxing in volume	the vivid green of the rainy season
scarce perceptible	ere it ceased to rage
the face of the earth	the mighty roar
miraculously saved	their hearts failing them

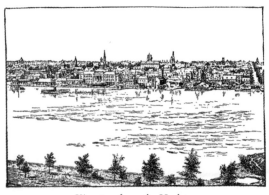

Kingston from the Harbour.

LESSON 4

GULLIVER IN LILLIPUT

Introduction.—In his *Gulliver's Travels* Swift makes Gulliver relate how he was shipwrecked and cast up on the coast of Lilliput, a country inhabited by the Lilliputians, a race of exceedingly small men. Many things in the following extract show how small they were. He was discovered by the Lilliputians asleep on the shore, and tied by a great number of their slender ropes to stakes driven into the ground. Later a chain strong enough to hold him was made, and he was brought to the capital. The Emperor of Lilliput had ordered two of his officers, Clefrin Frelock and Marsi Frelock, to make an inventory of the contents of Gulliver's pockets, and these are the two officers that Gulliver took up in his hands.

I TOOK up the two officers in my hands, put them first into my coat-pockets, and then into every other pocket about me, except my two fobs,[*] and another secret pocket wherein I had some little necessaries that were of no consequence to any but myself. In one of my fobs there was a silver watch, and in the other a small quantity of gold in a purse. These gentlemen, having pens, ink, and paper about them, made an exact inventory of everything they saw; and, when they had done, desired I would set them down, that they might deliver it to the emperor. This inventory I afterwards translated into English, and it is word for word as follows:

Imprimis,[†] In the right coat-pocket of the great man-mountain, after the strictest search, we found only one great piece of coarse cloth, large enough to be a foot-cloth

---

[*] Small pockets in the waistband of his trousers.
[†] A legal expression—"In the first place."

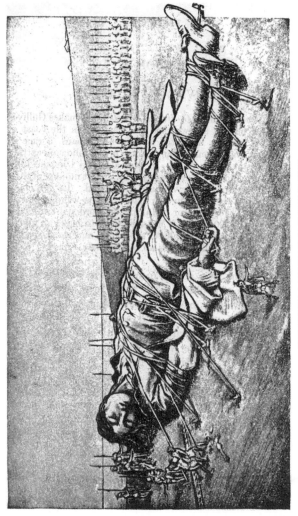

GULLIVER A PRISONER IN LILLIPUT.

for your Majesty's chief room of state. In the left pocket we saw a huge silver chest, with a cover of the same metal, which we, the searchers, were not able to lift. We desired it should be opened; and one of us stepping into it, found himself up to the knees in a sort of dust, some part whereof flying up to our faces, set us both sneezing for several times together.

In his right waistcoat-pocket we found a prodigious bundle of white, thin substance, about the bigness of three men, tied with a strong rope, and marked with black figures, which we humbly conceive to be writings, every letter almost half as large as the palm of our hands. In the left there was a sort of engine, from the back of which were extended twenty long poles, resembling the palisades before your Majesty's court, wherewith, we conjecture, the man-mountain combs his head; for we did not always trouble him with questions, because we found it a great difficulty to make him understand us.

In the large pocket on the right side of his middle cover, we saw a hollow pillar of iron, about the length of a man, fastened to a strong piece of timber larger than the pillar; and upon one side of the pillar were huge pieces of iron sticking out, cut into strange figures, which we knew not what to make of. In the left pocket, another engine of the same kind.

In the smaller pocket on the right side were several round, flat pieces of white and red metal, of different bulk. Some of the white, which seemed to be silver, were so large and heavy that my comrade and I could hardly lift them. In the left pocket were two black pillars, irregularly shaped. We could not without difficulty reach the top of them as we stood at the bottom of his pocket. One of them was covered, and seemed all of a piece; but at the upper end of the other there appeared a white, round substance, about twice the bigness of our heads. Within each of these was enclosed a prodigious plate of steel, which by our orders we obliged him to show us, because we apprehended they might be dangerous engines. He took them out of their cases, and told us that in his own country his practice was to shave his beard with one of these, and cut his meat with the other.

There were two pockets which we could not enter. These he called his fobs: they were two large slits cut into the tops of his middle cover, but squeezed close by the pressure of his body. Out of the right fob hung a great silver chain, with a wonderful kind of engine at the bottom. We directed him to draw out whatever was at the end of that chain, which appeared to be a globe, half silver and half of some transparent metal; for on the transparent side we saw certain strange figures circularly drawn, and thought we could touch them, till we found our fingers stopped by that lucid substance.

He put this engine to our ears, which made an incessant noise, like that of a water-mill; and we conjecture it is either some unknown animal or the god that he worships; but we are more inclined to the latter opinion, because he assured us (if we understand him right, for he expressed himself very imperfectly), that he seldom did anything without consulting it. He called it his oracle, and said it pointed out the time for every action of his life.

From the left fob he took out a net almost large enough for a fisherman, but contrived to open and shut like a purse. We found therein several massy pieces of yellow metal, which, if they be real gold, must be of immense value.

Having thus, in obedience to your Majesty's commands, diligently searched all his pockets, we observed a girdle about his waist made of the hide of some prodigious animal, from which on the left side hung a sword of the length of five men, and on the right a bag or pouch divided into two cells, each cell capable of holding three of your Majesty's subjects. In one of these cells were several globes or balls of a most ponderous metal, about the bigness of our heads; the other cell contained a heap of certain black grains, but of no great bulk or weight, for we could hold above fifty of them in the palms of our hands.

This is an exact inventory of what we found about the body of the man-mountain, who used us with great civility, and due respect to your Majesty's commission.

Signed and sealed on the fourth day of the eighty-ninth moon of your Majesty's auspicious reign.

CLEFRIN FRELOCK,
MARSI FRELOCK.

When this inventory was read over to the emperor, he directed me, although in very gentle terms, to deliver up the several particulars. He first called for my scimitar, which I took out, scabbard and all. In the meantime he ordered three thousand of the choicest troops (who then attended him) to surround me at a distance, with their bows and arrows just ready to discharge; but I did not observe it, for mine eyes were wholly fixed on His Majesty.

He then desired me to draw my scimitar, which, although it had got some rust by the sea-water, was in most parts exceedingly bright. I did so, and immediately all the troops gave a shout between terror and surprise; for the sun shone clear, and the reflection dazzled their eyes as I waved the scimitar to and fro in my hand. His Majesty, who is a most magnanimous prince, was less daunted than I could expect: he ordered me to return it into the scabbard, and cast it on the ground as gently as I could, about six feet from the end of my chain.

The next thing he demanded was one of the hollow iron pillars, by which he meant my pocket pistols. I drew it out, and at his desire, as well as I could, expressed to him the use of it; and charging it only with powder, which, by the closeness of my pouch, happened to escape wetting in the sea (an inconvenience against which all prudent mariners take special care to provide), I first cautioned the emperor not to be afraid, and then I let it off in the air. The astonishment here was much greater than at the sight of the scimitar. Hundreds fell down as if they had been struck dead; and even the emperor, although he stood his ground, could not recover himself for some time.

I delivered up both my pistols in the same manner as I had done my scimitar, and then my pouch of powder and bullets, begging him that the former might be kept from fire, for it would kindle with the slightest spark, and blow up his imperial palace into the air. I likewise delivered up my watch, which the emperor was very curious to see, and commanded two of his tallest yeomen of the guards to bear it on a pole upon their shoulders, as draymen in England do a barrel of ale. He was amazed at the continual noise it made, and the motion of the minute-hand, which he could easily discern, for their sight is much more acute than ours. He asked the opinions of his learned men about it, which were various and remote, as the reader may well imagine without my repeating; although. indeed, I could not very perfectly understand them. I then gave up my silver and copper money, my purse, with nine large pieces of gold and some smaller ones; my knife and razor, my comb and silver snuff-box, my handkerchief and journal-book. My scimitar, pistols, and pouch were conveyed in carriages to His Majesty's stores, but the rest of my goods were returned to me.

I had, as I before observed, one private pocket, which escaped their search, wherein there were a pair of spectacles (which I sometimes use for the weakness of mine eyes), and some other little conveniences; which, being of no consequence to the emperor, I did not think myself bound in honour to discover, and I apprehended they might be lost or spoiled if I ventured them out of my possession.

DEAN SWIFT.
From *Gulliver's Travels*.

[In the book from which this lesson was taken you may also read of Gulliver's adventures in the country of Brobdingnag, where the people were huge giants, so that Gulliver was to them what a Lilliputian had been to him.]

EXERCISES

1. Mention some of the things that show how small the Lilliputians were as compared with ordinary people.
2. How did the two officers describe:
   (*a*) Gulliver's watch?
   (*b*) His pistols?

(c) His snuff-box?

(d) His comb?

3. How do you know from the lesson (*not* the Introduction) that Gulliver was shipwrecked on the coast of Lilliput?

4. "Necessary" is usually an adjective. It may also be used as a noun, meaning a thing that is constantly needed. It is used thus in this lesson. Is it given in the singular or the plural? Write out the sentence containing it.

5. Which words in the lesson mean the same as the following:

    (a) a list of things with their descriptions?

    (b) very large or striking?

    (c) a strong fence of wooden or iron stakes?

    (d) guess?

    (e) ceaseless?

    (f) that may be seen through?

    (g) industrious?

6. Make a list of the twelve words which cause you the most difficulty to spell. Learn them thoroughly.

LESSON 5

THE LIVING PLANT—I

PLANTS are composed of various members, which are known as roots, stems, leaves, flowers, fruits, and seeds. Each member has its own particular work to do for the living plant, just as each part of the human body is essential for our life and proper growth. We will therefore learn what are the duties of the different parts of a plant, remembering that it sometimes happens that if one part is absent another part may perform its work.

ROOTS

The root is that part of the plant which usually grows downwards into the soil and sends out root branches in all directions. The two main functions of roots are: (1) to fix the plant firmly so that it cannot be blown down by the wind, and (2) to absorb water with mineral salts in solution, by means of which the plant is fed.

There are two distinct kinds of root systems; plants are usually known as either *tap-rooted* or *fibrous-rooted*. In the tap-rooted class the primary root thrusts its way downwards into the ground, forming what is known as a tap root. From this tap root large numbers of root branches are produced, and they ramify through the soil in all directions in search of food. Trees, shrubs, and herbs belong to this system, well-known examples being the mango, the orange, the cotton-plant, the ochro, the lettuce, beans, and the tobacco-plant.

In the fibrous-rooted class there is no definite tap root, but we find instead a cluster of root branches produced directly from the base of the stem. Palms, bamboos, corn, and other grasses have roots of this character.

You may readily observe and study these two different forms of root systems by germinating some seeds of beans and of corn at the side of a glass jar filled with soil.

Roots absorb their food by means of minute hairs which grow on the very young rootlets. Water is sucked in by these root hairs and taken through the main roots to the stem and thence to other parts of the plant. The tip of each rootlet is protected by a root-cap, which enables it to push through hard soil without injury.

In a well-drained soil the rain passes through, leaving a film of water covering each tiny particle of soil, ready to be absorbed by the root hairs. If the soil is not properly drained, air, which is also necessary for the healthy growth of the roots, cannot enter.

Apart from their ordinary work, roots sometimes take on special functions. Sometimes they act as storehouses for the food of plants, as in the case of the cassava, the radish, the turnip, and the beetroot. In tropical forests many plants may be seen climbing by means of their roots, which grow out from their stems and cling firmly to the trunks of trees. Well-known root climbers are the vanilla and various plants which belong to the same family as the tannia and the dasheen.

Some plants, such as tree orchids, have clinging roots by which they fasten themselves on to trees, but these plants also produce feeding roots, which penetrate into the decaying vegetable matter and dust around the plant, and thus absorb soluble plant foods. Orchids also have aerial roots which take in through their tips some of the water which trickles down them.

The matapalo or "Scotch Attorney" is a well-known example of a tree with aerial roots. We read in Book IV. how its seeds usually germinate in the forks of trees, from whence they send aerial roots to the ground, often many feet below, and these become anchored in the soil and develop a normal underground root system. The mangrove is another common instance of a tree with roots of this kind. You may have seen how in this inhabitant of the swamps the roots reach from the branches to the ground and act as a support to them.

STEMS

The stem of a plant is that portion which bears buds, leaves, flowers, and fruits, although these may not all be present at the same time. In some cases one or more of these members may be absent altogether.

Stems generally grow above the ground, but some plants, such as the ginger, the banana, and the arrowroot, have stems which grow and remain underground. These plants only send their leaves and leaf-stalks up into the air. Sometimes they develop above ground what is apparently a stem, as in the case of the banana, but on examination you will find that the so-called stem is only the tightly rolled bases of the leaves.

Aerial Roots of Mangrove.

Stems have two chief functions: in the first place they serve as a support to the leaves, flowers, and fruit, usually sending out branches in all directions to enable these members to get as much sunlight as possible; secondly, they are the channel by which the raw food in solution is conveyed from the roots to the leaves, where it undergoes changes or is manufactured before being sent back through them to the various growing points or plant storehouses.

Climbing Stems of Lianes or "Tie-ties".

There are many kinds of stems. Some grow large, woody, and erect, as in the timber trees of the forest; others, such as annuals,* are slender and easily damaged. There are climbing stems of many varieties, some, such as the lianes, even reaching to the tops of tall trees, whilst on the other hand there are stems which creep along the ground like those of the sweet potato.

Many underground stems are really storehouses where the plant stores up supplies of food for future use. The ginger and the arrowroot are examples of this class. Yams and tannias also are really underground stems of this kind; they differ from roots by bearing buds. If you cut either of these into pieces and plant them, each bud will produce shoots and leaves.

* See Lesson 34.

The stem storehouses of plants, both aerial and underground, are often of great use and value to man, and are the sources of many of our principal foods. Well-known examples are the sugar-cane, the arrowroot, the yam, and the potato.

A cactus plant

Cactus plants, which grow in dry places, are adapted to their surroundings by having stems which store up a reserve of water to enable the plant to exist in times of drought.

EXERCISES

1. The word *minute* can be pronounced in two distinct ways. Its meaning changes with the change of pronunciation. What does it mean in each of the following cases?

Word.	Pronunciation.	Meaning.
minute	min´-it	....
minute	min-ūt´	....

2. What are the ordinary uses of roots? Make a list of special duties they sometimes perform, giving an example in each case.

3. *Aër* is Latin for "air." What is meant, therefore, by *aerial* roots? What other words do you know which begin with *aer*? Why are sweet drinks known as *aerated* waters?

4. What are the ordinary uses of stems? Make a list of special duties they sometimes perform, giving an example in each case.

5. Make sentences of your own containing these words :

composed	protected	germinate
essential	absorbed	anchored
functions	penetrate	inhabitant
definite	soluble	apparently

6. Fill in the blanks:

(a) A plant is a _____ thing, although it does not _____ about rapidly or _____ a noise. It lives its own _____, and at the same time does things which animals _____ do. It even _____ its own food by means of its leaves.

(b) Plants, like all _____, require _____, _____, and _____, but we do not see them eating, _____, or breathing, because we do not look in the right way.

(c) The _____ of every root is _____ with a little cap, or_____, which _____ it from injury. It may often be _____ in roots _____ in water, as, for example, in those of the _____ _____, of which we read in Book IV.

(d) Stems like _____ often serve as _____ houses of food. The _____ _____ stores up a large _____ of sugar in its stem, whilst the underground _____ of the _____ stores up starch.

THE BOYHOOD OF RALEIGH. (*Sir John Everett Millais, P.R.A.*)

LESSON 6

PICTURE LESSONS—I

THE BOYHOOD OF RALEIGH

A WRITER who wishes to make a strong impression upon his readers must be careful about two things: he must select the best words for his purpose, and he must arrange his sentences with great care.

In just the same way an artist must not only draw the various parts of his picture as well as he can, but he must put these parts together so that each one helps the others to make a perfect whole.

This "Boyhood of Raleigh" was painted by Sir John Millais, a celebrated English artist.

The boys (Walter Raleigh and his half-brother Humphrey Gilbert) are listening eagerly to a sunburnt sailor, who has just returned from the wilds of the scarcely known America, with such tales of wrecks and of fighting with the Spaniards, and such descriptions of the wonders to be seen on shore, that the two boys are spellbound, as you can see. Already in imagination they are in the midst of these wonders. Nothing will afterwards be able to turn their thoughts from "Westward Ho" and the magic of its call.

Well, that is the story or the central idea of the famous painting. Let us see how the artist has dealt with it.

When an artist is young he learns how great pictures are put together, or, as we say, *composed*. He finds that there are many lines and lights and colours that help each other if well placed, and that other lines and colours would not go so well together.

As the artist grows more expert in putting a picture together, he does not have to think of these things in a conscious way or to follow definite rules like a mathematician or scientist. By that time he composes by *feeling* that certain lines and colours go well together. But I do not think that he would be likely to do so unless he had studied to find such lines in other men's paintings when he was young.

The rough sketch on this page will show you what I mean. You see that the sailor and the boys are enclosed by

a big curved line, so as to concentrate attention on the human group and especially on the rapt face of Raleigh, and that curves can be imagined to join other parts of the picture. There are dozens of others you can find for yourself.

Now, though Millais probably did not think of many of these lines, his *feeling* would have told him when the parts of the picture did not fall together, and then he would discover that these could be improved by shifting an arm or a whole figure, so that it should *compose* more finely with the other parts.

In the first place, he wishes to draw our attention immediately to the two boys, and especially to their faces. So he places them looking towards us, and near the middle of the picture.

Then, again, the sailor raises his left arm so that the hand points towards the boys, and therefore carries our eyes in that direction.

See, too, how the top of the sea-wall is drawn just on the level of the boys' heads; and as a long line anywhere in a picture attracts attention, perhaps without our knowing it, so this sea-wall plays its part in fixing our eyes on the boys' faces.

LESSON 7

IRON AND STEEL

Of all the metals known to man, iron is one of the most widely distributed and is the most useful. Next to the air we breathe, the water we drink, and the food we eat, iron is the most necessary of all substances. As civilized men we simply could not do without it. In the form of cast iron, wrought iron, or steel, it is the basis of almost everything which must be made strong and enduring.

Ancient Greek stories tell us of an "old man of the sea" named Proteus, who had the power of changing himself into all sorts of shapes, and thus was able to baffle those who tried to secure him. Iron may be called the Proteus of metals, for it can take an almost infinite variety of forms and characters.

You have only to look around you to see what an enormous number of things are made of iron. Suppose you are in your kitchen. You see that the coal-pot is made of iron, and that most of the pots and pans which are used for cooking are constructed of the same metal. Knives and forks, ladles, dish covers, locks, door handles, and the nails which hold woodwork together, all consist of iron or steel, either in part or in whole.

Many buildings are now constructed of an iron or steel skeleton, upon which the stone or concrete work is built; in the tropics we roof our houses and other buildings with galvanized iron, which is merely sheet iron covered with a thin layer of zinc to prevent it from rusting. Ships are made of steel; so, too, are all kinds of engines and the machinery in our sugar factories. The rails on which our locomotives run consist of steel. The pipes which convey water from the reservoirs to our houses are made of iron, as also are the lamp-posts in our streets, the railings round our savannahs, and a thousand other things that meet our eyes at every turn. It has been well said that iron is the soul of manufacture and the mainspring of civilized life.

Then consider what different characters iron may take. It may be so hard and strong as to be almost unbreakable, or it may be as brittle as glass. It may be so tough that it can scarcely be stretched, or it may be drawn out into wire as easily as copper. It may be springy or lifeless, and it may be made so hard and sharp that it will cut and shape almost every other metal.

It may be welded easily, or scarcely at all; it may be turned readily into a liquid, or be so treated that it can only be melted by the intensest heat. It may conduct electricity freely or with difficulty. There is scarcely a single property which iron cannot be made to assume.

Iron is usually found in the earth as an ore, mixed with other substances, from which it must be freed before it is fit for working. In appearance the ore resembles lumps of rock or stone. Iron ore often occurs in what are called the Coal Measures; in some places it is so largely mingled with coaly matter that it can be smelted without any other fuel. The great hardware industries of Britain have arisen because the mother-country has an abundance of coal and iron ore, and because both are found together, or not far away from each other.

Iron ores which contain little of other substances are found in parts of England, in the Irish bogs, and in districts of France, Germany, Sweden, and Canada. The ordinary ores are first heated in kilns, in order to drive off moisture and certain gases. They are then taken to the blast furnace, and are mixed with a certain amount of coke and limestone.

People who live near the coalfields are quite familiar with the blast furnace, for it is a pillar of cloud by day and a pillar of fire by night. You can imagine what they are like from the picture on the next page. The blast furnace is a hollow tower from sixty to ninety feet high, lined with fire-brick and cased with steel plates. A fire is lighted at the bottom of the furnace, and the mixture of iron, coke, and limestone is emptied in from a gallery at the top.

A hot blast of air is forced into the furnace, and the intense heat thus raised melts the iron from the ore. The impurities float on the surface, and form the slag or waste product, like the mud from the cane-juice, of which you will read in Lesson 38, while the iron streams out into a number of sand moulds. When it cools it is "pig iron", so called because the sand gutters into which it flows are supposed to resemble a sow and her pigs.

TAPPING A BLAST FURNACE.

Here are verses which are put into the mouth of the ironmaster:

"I take my toll of the hard-won coal
  For my greedy furnace high;
Hear the fierce blast roar as it melts the ore,
  While the flames leap to the sky.

See! hour by hour its fiery power
  Never slackens in fierce affray,
Till in hissing steam, with a ruddy gleam
  Good metal flows away."

The metal which flows away may be "good metal" from the point of view of the ironmaster, but it is not yet ready for the manufacturer. The "pig iron" thus obtained is hard, brittle, and not difficult to melt. It contains carbon and other substances, and some of these impurities must be removed before the iron will bend and serve the needs of those who work it up into various forms.

This may be done by putting the pig iron into what is called a puddling furnace, where it is heated greatly; the iron is thus melted again, and some of the impurities are driven off in the form of gases. The iron is next made up into balls, which are hammered in order to remove the slag; they are then rolled into bars, which are again cut up and reheated, and finally rolled once more into the form needed. The wrought iron thus produced is tough, and can be hammered out or drawn into wire.

Steel is the most useful form of iron. It can be made of such hardness that it will cut through almost any substance, or become so flexible as to bend like a bow. Further, it can be drawn out into wires of great strength and elasticity.

The armour-plate of men-of-war, big guns, tools, weapons, and parts of such huge pieces of machinery as rolling mills, steam hammers, and lathes for cutting and shaping hard metals, are all made of steel.

Steel is made by combining with iron a certain quantity of carbon, which never amounts to more than two parts in a hundred, together with other substances. What is called mild steel contains less carbon than tool steel. Mild steel is now the most valuable material known to industry, and has taken the place of wrought iron. What are called tin-plates are made of mild steel coated with tin.

Let me tell you the way in which mild steel is made by the Bessemer process. If you could visit one of the great steelworks in Sheffield, you would be shown a pear-shaped vessel of mild steel, lined with firebricks and furnished with a big spout. It is so mounted that it can easily be raised or lowered, and tipped so that the contents can be poured out in a stream. This vessel is known as a converter.

Pig iron is melted and run into the converter; then a strong blast of air is sent through the fluid mass. The result is that the metal is swiftly brought to an intense heat, and is freed from impurity. Out of the mouth of the converter rush a myriad sparks and brilliant tongues of flame. In the depths of the vessel the molten metal bubbles and tosses, and shows most beautiful tints of crimson, blue, and gold.

Close by, in the blinding glare, stand the steel-workers, watching for the exact moment to shut off the air-blast. Should they continue it too long or cut it off too soon, they will probably spoil the material. When they see the flame drop they know that all the carbon has been removed.

A blast furnace.

Then in the nick of time they lower the converter, and add a preparation containing, in the right proportion, those elements which will turn the molten metal into steel.

The converter is now tipped, and its contents, white as driven snow, flow into a ladle and are cast into ingots. These ingots are used in the manufacture of rails, girders, cranks, wheels, boilers, marine-engine shafts, and many articles of industrial and household use.

The best steel, such as is used for motor cars, aeroplanes, and warships, is now made by another method, known as the "open hearth" process, whilst tool steels have to be hardened by being heated red-hot and suddenly plunged into water.

EXERCISES

1. In what other place have you read of "a pillar of cloud by day and a pillar of fire by night"? What does this expression mean?

2. Which words in the lesson mean the same as the following:

    (a) lasting,   (f) a place where water is stored,
    (b) without end,   (g) joined together,
    (c) made of,   (h) iron and steel manufactures,
    (d) framework,   (i) to have a similar appearance,
    (e) engines,   (j) 2 per cent.?

3. Make two lists showing the things named in the lesson as being made of (i.) iron, and (ii.) steel. Can you add four more names to each list?

4. Why are iron and steel goods not made in large quantities in the West Indies? Are any such articles made here? If so, where? Name them.

5. What is the difference between iron and steel? What is "galvanized iron"? (Remember that the name is not "galvanize"; this word is a verb, not a noun.)

6. Explain why all West Indian children should know something about iron and steel, although iron ore is not found in our countries.

LESSON 8

SPANISH WATERS

Introduction.—An old pirate, or buccaneer, is supposed to be speaking in this poem. He longs to be back on the Spanish Main, at the spot—Los Muertos (a Spanish name meaning "the dead")—where the pirates have hidden their treasure in the deathly mangrove swamps or marshes.

SPANISH waters, Spanish waters, you are ringing in my ears,
Like a slow, sweet piece of music from the grey forgotten years;
Telling tales, and beating tunes, and bringing weary thoughts
      to me
Of the sandy beach at Muertos, where I would that I could be.

There's a surf breaks on Los Muertos, and it never stops to roar,
And it's there we came to anchor, and it's there we went ashore,
Where the blue lagoon is silent amid snags of rotting trees,
Dropping like the clothes of corpses cast up by the seas.

We anchored at Los Muertos when the dipping sun was red,
We left her half-a-mile to sea, to west of Nigger Head;
And before the mist was on the Cay, before the day was done,
We were all ashore on Muertos with the gold that we had won.

We bore it through the marshes in a half-score battered chests,
Sinking, in the sucking quagmires, to the sunburn on our
      breasts,
Heaving over tree-trunks, gasping, damning at the flies and heat,
Longing for a long drink, out of silver, in the ship's cool lazareet.[*]

The moon came white and ghostly as we laid the treasure down,
There was gear there'd make a beggarman as rich as Lima Town,

---

[*] The ship's hospital.

Copper charms and silver trinkets from the chests of Spanish crews,
Gold doubloons and double moidores, louis-d'ors and portagues,*

Clumsy yellow-metal earrings from the Indians of Brazil,
Uncut emeralds out of Rio, bezoar† stones from Guayaquil;
Silver, in the crude and fashioned, pots of old Arica bronze,
Jewels from the bones of Incas desecrated by the Dons.

We smoothed the place with mattocks, and we took and blazed
    the tree
Which marks yon where the gear is hid that none will ever see,
And we laid aboard the ship again, and south away we steers,
Through the loud surf of Los Muertos which is beating in my ears.

   .   .   .   .   .   .

JOHN MASEFIELD.
From *Ballads and Poems,* by permission of the Author and
Messrs. Elkin Matthews.

EXERCISES

1. Quote the expressions from the poem which give the death-like atmosphere of Los Muertos.
2. Where had the treasure been obtained?
3. Who were the following: the Dons, the Incas, the Indians, and the Spanish crews?
4. Find these places on the map: Lima, Brazil, Rio, and Guayaquil.
5. Express the following phrases in another way:—the grey forgotten years; when the dipping sun was red; clumsy yellow-metal earrings; blazed the tree; where the gear is hid; laid aboard the ship.
6. Scan each line of the first verse. How many feet are there? Which foot in each line is incomplete?

* Names of various coins.
† A stone formerly thought to be an antidote to all poisons.

LESSON 9

FOOD

IN Book IV. we learned that air and water are absolutely necessary for life, and in this lesson we shall see that food also is equally important, for without food living things could not grow, their waste or used-up matter could not be replaced, and they must die.

All parts of our body are doing work at one time or another, and in the process we are always burning up, so to speak. Even the act of thinking, which, though very hard work for some of us, is often regarded as not being work at all, is so much work done, with energy consumed and its consequent wastage of tissue. Like a steam-engine, therefore, the human body thus requires food or fuel to keep it in a healthy and active condition.

But the process of nourishing the body is a very complicated affair, on account of the differences in structure and function of the various tissues (skin, bones, muscles, nerves, and blood) of which it is composed. In addition, the body possesses the remarkable property of manufacturing for itself the new parts required for its growth.

The material from which these different parts and tissues are built as we grow, and are replaced when worn out by use, and from which also they get the power to carry out their various activities, can only come from the food we eat. It is important, therefore, to know the kinds of food which our bodies require. Generally speaking, they may be classified as follows:

(a) *Body-building Foods.*—Substances from which the tissues are built up during growth in childhood and which replace waste in later life.

(b) *Energy- and Heat-producing Foods.*—Substances which, like the fuel of the steam-engine, supply warmth and the power to do work.

(c) *Protective or Purifying Foods.*—Substances valuable for the *vitamins* which they contain, and which are essential for growth and health.

(d) *Water.*

Body-building Foods.—The different organs and tissues of our bodies are made up of a countless number of small units or cells, which may be likened to bricks building up the human house. These cells differ in many respects, but are all alike in containing a substance named *protoplasm* (Greek, *protos,* first, and *plasma,* form), which is the basis of all living matter. An important constituent of protoplasm is nitrogen, of which you read in the lesson on "Air."

Nitrogen is thus essential to life, and for this reason the substances which supply nitrogen are named *proteins* (*protos,* first). Proteins have been named "the building-stones of tissues," because, after being broken down into their simple elements by the digestive juices, they pass through the intestinal canal and recombine to form the various proteins that the different tissues use. Just as in architecture stones, wood, and other materials are shaped by workmen to build in one case an ordinary house, or in another a large and beautiful cathedral, so in the case of our bodies food proteins are broken down and reformed to build up the different tissue proteins required by the skin, bones, muscles, nerves, and blood.

Proteins are readily obtained from the flesh of animals, fish, fresh milk, eggs, cheese, and also from pulse foods such as peas, beans, lentils, corn, flour (wheat), and rice. Just as some building materials are of better quality than others, so do these proteins or tissue-builders vary in quality—meat, milk, and certain kinds of fish representing the better values.

Another class of substances—salts or mineral matter required for bones and teeth—comes under this head. These things are plentifully present in milk, vegetables, and fruit. In many vegetables and fruits also there are fibrous materials which are useful in stimulating movements of the bowels.

Energy- and Heat-producing Foods.—Our bodies are never entirely at rest, and for health and comfort must be kept warm. Every movement at play or work means expenditure of energy, and this can only take place if the proper kind of fuel or food is supplied. These energy-producing foods are represented by two classes of substances, (*a*) sugars and starches, and (*b*) fats. They are both composed of the chemical elements, carbon, hydrogen, and oxygen.

Sugars and starches, termed *carbohydrates,* occur in all sugars and cereals, and in vegetables, particularly root vegetables, oatmeal, rice, flour (wheat), potatoes, breadfruit, bananas, yams, and other ground provisions. Fats are present in beef, mutton, pork, fish, milk, butter, cream, cheese, and also in the oil of plants such as olives, groundnuts, and palms.

Vitamins.—These substances occur in minute quantities in various foods, and are essential for keeping the body in good condition and giving it the power to resist disease.

They are all products of the plant world, and when present in animal tissues are always derived from vegetable food. One kind originates in green leaves, and when these are eaten by an animal the vitamin is stored in its fat. Thus the fat in cow's milk contains the vitamin because the cow eats grass.

Vitamins are found especially in fresh milk, green vegetables such as lettuce and cabbage, carrots, fresh fruit such as oranges, limes, and lemons, bran of wheat used in whole-meal bread, yeast, and brown or unpolished rice. They are destroyed by the bleaching of flour and the preservation of food by means of salt, canning, or drying. They are thus absent from tinned milk.

When there is a lack of vitamins in food certain diseases are apt to develop, such as marasmus in children, and scurvy among sailors who make long voyages when preserved foods only are available.

Water.—Food substances can only reach the tissues in solution—that is, by water transport. Water is also essential for the removal of waste products. Most food substances contain a large proportion of water, but our bodies require a good deal of water, and this should be taken freely when we are thirsty, except during meals, when it may interfere with the proper mastication of the food.

.   .   .   .   .   .

Although it is convenient to group the various kinds of food into these classes, it must be borne in mind that the classes are not quite distinct. Thus proteins, while mainly composed of proteid matter, also contain fats; similarly carbohydrates also contain proteid matter, and vitamins occur in a wide variety of food substances.

It is not good to attempt to live on one kind of food alone. If only bread and butter were eaten, though these would provide plenty of starch and fat, it would be necessary to consume a large quantity of this food in order to obtain enough of the body-building substance, protein. Meat furnishes a great deal of protein, but no starch. Again, if fresh vegetables or fruit are not included in the diet, a sufficiency of vitamins, salts, and acids is lacking. It is best to eat a little of a good many different kinds of food, and generally the plainer the food the better.

Nutrition is not merely a matter of putting so much protein, carbohydrates, and fats into our stomachs. The food must be digested and absorbed by the cells of our tissues, and this assimilation depends on the healthy working of the several organs and parts of the body. Fresh air, exercise, rest, and the removal of waste products all play important parts in the maintenance of health.

The conditions under which food is eaten have a good deal to do with the benefit the body derives from it. Its preparation is important; good cooking makes it attractive and palatable, and helps digestion.

Considerations of Quantity and Quality of Food.— The following points should be noted:

1. *Age.*—It is generally accepted that if the quantity of food required by an adult is represented by 100, a young child requires 50, between six and ten years it needs 70, between ten and fourteen years, 80. Boys and girls over fourteen require as much as an adult.

2. *Climate.*—Less protein and fat and more green vegetables and fruit are required in hot climates than in cold.

3. *Freshness.*—Food should be as fresh as possible. The best meat is fresh meat, the best fish is fish recently caught, and the best milk is clean cool milk fresh from the cow.

Strict cleanliness in the preparation and handling of food is very necessary, and especial care should be taken to keep food, particularly milk, covered in a cool place and protected from dust and flies.

There is no perfect food. Milk is the nearest approach to a perfect food, but it lacks some indigestible material to act as a stimulant to the bowels.

In selecting a diet the chief points to keep in mind are these:

1. A sufficient supply of body-building food or protein.
2. A supply of vegetables, some of which should be *green* vegetables.
3. Whenever practicable, some fresh milk should be included.

EXERCISES

1. Explain why everything that is eaten is not necessarily "food."
2. What are the different classes of foods? Give some examples of West Indian foods in each class.
3. What are vitamins? Where do they originate? Of what value are they?
4. Why is polished rice of less value as a food than unpolished rice?
5. Explain why food without water would be of little or no use to the body, however good it might be in itself.
6. Why is fresh milk the best food for infants?
7. Make out a suitable diet for the meals of three consecutive days. Give reasons for including each article.

BENBOW CONTINUED TO DIRECT THE FIGHT.

(*See page 61.*)

LESSON 10

BENBOW THE BRAVE

Introduction.—Kipling has said, "What should they know of England who only England know?" This might well be applied to the West Indies, for in order to understand thoroughly the part they play in the affairs of the world, it is necessary to have a knowledge of things and events in lands far afield. This fact is especially true when studying West Indian history, as the early story of our islands, from the fifteenth to the eighteenth century, was largely determined by happenings elsewhere.

We saw in Book IV. that, soon after their discovery, the Pope solemnly bestowed practically all the lands in the New World on Spain. When, therefore, in 1580, Portugal and the Portuguese possession of Brazil were also annexed by Spain, the Spanish claim to a monopoly of the New World and its trade seemed complete. From the time of Columbus, however, that claim had not been admitted by the kings of France and England, and towards the end of the sixteenth century the Dutch, who had revolted from Spain, also disputed it.

After the defeat of the Spanish Armada by the English navy, the power of Spain began to wane, and it was as much as she could do to retain possession of the larger islands and the parts of the mainland where she held sway. During the seventeenth century England wrested Jamaica from her, and both England and France formed settlements in several of the smaller islands. The mistress of the seas at this time, however, as far as commerce was concerned, was undoubtedly Holland. In her hands was all the carrying trade of the world.

The eighteenth century saw a prolonged struggle between England and France, the real object of which was to settle the two questions: Who was to be master in the New World? and, Who was to create an Indian empire? Whenever we find the two nations at war in Europe we find just as keen a conflict raging in other places where their interests clashed, and it is to this fact that the many changes in ownership of certain West Indian islands between the years 1700 and 1800 are due.

The three chief actors on the scene of the West Indian stage during that century were therefore the English, French, and Dutch. We find these are all represented here to-day, as the islands of Guadeloupe and Martinique, in addition to Cayenne, or French Guiana, on the mainland, remain in the possession of France, whilst Holland retained Curacao off the coast of Venezuela, and Surinam or Dutch Guiana. Many were the stirring episodes which occurred in the struggles between these nations in our lands and on our seas during those early days.

ONE of the most popular of the naval heroes whose doughty deeds in the Caribbean will be remembered for ever was the rough and hearty old Admiral Benbow. He was the idol of his men, but his unpolished and boisterous manners were not so endearing to the officers who served under him.

Some say that he was the son of a tanner of Shrewsbury; others declare that his father was a butcher; but whichever is correct, there is little doubt of the fact that while still a boy he ran away to sea and joined the navy. His manners were therefore not likely to be improved by his early training, and this possibly accounted for an incident later at Jamaica, when, as admiral, he treated "a little briskly" the captains of various ships then serving under his command, and this was afterwards the direct cause of conduct by his captains which led to the most disgraceful episode in the annals of the British navy.

Young Benbow's early years were passed partly in the navy and partly in the merchant service. In the latter his career was most adventurous, and the story is told how, on one occasion, when in command of a vessel trading to the Mediterranean, he captured a powerful Moorish pirate vessel after a tremendous engagement, during which the pirates twice boarded and all but carried his ship. Benbow's fierce courage, however, so animated his crew that ere long the pirates were glad to scramble back into their own ship, leaving on Benbow's deck thirteen of their number dead. He ordered their heads to be cut off and preserved in a tub of pork pickle, and took them to the astonished magistrate at Cadiz, from whom he demanded a reward.

Soon afterwards he re-entered the navy, and in 1697 was appointed commander-in-chief of the king's ships in the West Indies, with instructions to suppress piracy in the Caribbean Sea. Reaching Barbados in February 1698, and finding all quiet there, he at once proceeded to Cartagena on the Spanish Main. By threats of a blockade he persuaded the governor of that city to release two English ships which he was detaining there.

Benbow then went after the pirates, whom he hunted relentlessly, spreading consternation in their ranks. Some took refuge under the Danish flag at St. Thomas, while others left West Indian waters altogether, only to return when he sailed again for England in 1700, where he remained for but a brief spell, as he was once again destined to visit the West Indies.

War with France broke out afresh in 1701, and there was need of an able commander of the fleet in the Caribbean. The choice fell on Benbow, and he hoisted his flag on the *Breda*, a vessel of 70 guns, and sailed for the West Indies in August of that year. He arrived at Barbados on the 3rd of November, and finding the Leeward Islands in a good state of defence, he proceeded to Jamaica. While there he heard that a French force of superior strength to his own had arrived at Martinique, and later that a Spanish squadron had joined the French, and that the combined fleet had put to sea under Admiral du Casse, so he immediately decided to act on the offensive.

For a while he cruised off Haiti (Hispaniola), when, receiving word that Du Casse had sailed for Porto Bello, he went on the track of the French squadron in that direction. On the 19th of August, off Santa Marta, now a busy port in Colombia from which millions of bananas are shipped every year, the enemy were sighted, four ships of from 60 to 70 guns apiece, one of 30 to 40, a transport, three small armed vessels, and a sloop. Benbow had seven sail: one, his flagship, the *Breda,* of 70 guns, another of 64, one of 54, and four of 48 guns.

As the two squadrons drew within effective range a few broadsides were exchanged, and then the *Defiance* (64) and the *Windsor* (48) luffed up out of gunshot, leaving the *Breda* exposed to a heavy fire from the two rearmost ships of the French. The action continued till dark, but the *Breda* kept near the enemy all night, determined to bring on the action afresh next day.

On the morning of the 20th, at daybreak, the *Breda* and the *Ruby* (48) were almost within range of the enemy, a light breeze blowing, and the rest of the English squadron far astern. In the afternoon the wind freshened, and the Frenchmen, clapping on all the sail they could carry, drew off, not venturing to attack. The *Breda* and the *Ruby,* firing their bow chasers, pursued closely till the 23rd, when the latter, disabled, had to make for Port Royal to refit. About eight that night the other vessels of the squadron came up, having so far rendered no assistance whatsoever. The enemy was then only two miles ahead, and Benbow, now confident of bringing him to action, crowded on sail in chase and rapidly drew on the Frenchmen; but to his cruel disappointment every one of his ships, except the *Falmouth* (48), again dropped astern.

At 2 a.m. on the 24th the *Breda* came up with the enemy's sternmost ship and at once opened a heavy fire. The fight continued all night and the next day; and by evening, under the ceaseless pounding of the gallant *Breda,* a 70-gun ship of the enemy was reduced to a complete wreck, her rigging cut to pieces and her sails all gone. But the *Breda* and her crew had not gone scathless through the action; an hour after its commencement a chain shot shattered Benbow's right leg—a dreadful wound. As it was being dressed, one of his lieutenants, coming below, expressed his sorrow.

"I would rather have lost both legs," answered Benbow, "than have seen this dishonour brought on the English nation. But, do you hear, if another shot should take me off, behave like brave men and fight it out!" Then, unconquered by pain and loss of blood, Benbow had himself carried up to the quarter-deck, where, seated in a chair, with his mangled leg supported in a cradle, he continued to direct the fight.

The enemy now bore down to support and rescue their disabled consort, whereupon three of the English ships ran to leeward of the crippled Frenchman, fired their broadsides, and stood off to the south. The *Defiance* also fired part of her broadside into the disabled ship, which returned the fire; whereupon the *Defiance* put her helm a-weather and bore away before the wind, paying no heed to the signal for "close action" flying on the admiral's ship. Then the whole French squadron fell on and battered the *Breda*, till finally Benbow was forced to haul out of action in order to refit.

In a few hours, by dint of extraordinary exertions, the *Breda's* crew had her again in sufficient trim to renew the fight, and with undaunted pluck Benbow gave the order to continue the pursuit. Besides flying the signal for battle, he sent by boat a message to each captain requesting him to keep his line and to behave like a man. But to no purpose. Captain Kirkby of the *Defiance* came on board the *Breda* and told Benbow that "he had better desist; the French were very strong, and from what had passed he might guess that he could make nothing of it." The admiral was astounded, but sent for the other captains, who not only agreed with Kirkby, but joined him in signing a paper to that effect. Then poor Benbow, broken in heart, was forced to relinquish the pursuit and return to Jamaica.

It is said that the French admiral, Du Casse, on arriving at Cartagena, sent to Benbow the following letter:

"Sir,—I had little hopes on Monday last but to have supped in your cabin; it pleased God to order it otherwise, and I am thankful for it. As for those cowardly captains who deserted you, hang them up, for they deserve it. Yours, Du Casse."

Certainly the epithet "cowardly" was richly deserved by the captains of the English ships. They were brought to court-martial at Jamaica. One died before his trial began, two were shot, one imprisoned, and two others suspended.

Their whole conduct during the fight was infamous. Yet one and all had, time and again, proved themselves to be brave men. The fact was that Benbow's rough manners had so jarred and offended them that they had formed the resolution to refuse to fight under him.

EXERCISES

1. You have read the names of some of Benbow's fleet. How many of his ships are not named in this lesson? How many guns did they carry?

2.   "Come all you sailors bold,
         Lend an ear, lend an ear;
    Come all you sailors bold, lend an ear.
        'Tis of our admiral's fame,
        Brave Benbow call'd by name;
        How he fought on the Main
        You shall hear, you shall hear."
                  (*From an old Sea Chanty.*)

    Try to make one or more verses, with this as a model, to continue the chanty, or sailors' song. Bring in something about the fight.

3. Make a list of the names of places mentioned in this lesson. Find them on the map. How many are in the West Indies or immediate neighbourhood?

4. Explain what is meant by "What should they know of England who only England know?" Illustrate your answer by reference to the West Indies.

5. In what ways did Benbow show bravery? Why does Benbow excite our sympathy if not always our admiration?

6. Describe the fight in the words of
    (*a*) an English sailor,
    (*b*) a French sailor.
    Study the picture on page 56, and it will help you to supply details.

LESSON 11

SOME INTERESTING FACTS OF ANIMAL LIFE

Monkeys

Monkeys are of many varieties. They vary greatly both in structure and in appearance. Some are ornamental, others

Prehensile Tail.

are hideous. Although most are intelligent, a few are stupid. There are silent monkeys, chattering monkeys, and howling monkeys.

As you learned in Book II., many New World monkeys have exceedingly long prehensile tails, which serve as a fifth hand, while other monkeys have no tails at all. Some Old World monkeys have cheek pouches formed by folds in the skin, which may act as receptacles for carrying food, but when empty lie flat on the side of the face. The limbs of monkeys also vary greatly in length, but the arms are never longer than the legs, except in the man-like apes.

Some species of monkeys, among which are the South American spider-monkeys, have only an apology for a thumb. This digit is replaced by a mere knob, and it is supposed to have become so through disuse, for these creatures employ their hands simply as hooks. The lack of the thumb has one drawback from the monkey's point of view, for the spider-monkeys are unable to join other kinds of monkeys in their favourite sport of salt-hunting. You have seen these animals engaged in the ceaseless search of their own and their

Salt-hunting.

neighbours' coats; the object of the chase is not vermin, but the salty particles which clog their fur. Monkeys, like most animals, are very fond of salt.

As a result of constant use as a "fifth hand" the under surface of the tail of the spider-monkey has become quite hairless. These South American monkeys are very gentle when in captivity—in fact, they make charming pets; but they are far from docile in their native jungles on the Main, where huge troops swing through the tree-tops, ravaging birds' nests and pillaging the hives of bees and wasps.

A very entertaining creature is the bulky black-faced "woolly monkey" of Brazil, which takes its name from its woolly coat. It has a tail even longer than that of the spider-monkey, and may sometimes be seen accepting gifts and transferring them to its mouth by means of this appendage.

The Cat Family

There are about fifty species of this family, ranging in size from the lion or tiger down to the domestic cat. Apart from size, however, all cats are very similar in general structure and habits. They present a striking range of colouring, to suit the varied conditions of their natural abodes.

The Lion.

The lion in its brownish coat roams over the plains of Africa and Persia to India, while the tiger finds its stripes a great advantage among the dense bush of the jungle in India, Burma, and Sumatra. There its bold stripe-pattern melts into the background of tall bright stems and dark shadows, making it almost invisible.

For the first year of its life the young lion cub is spotted, and it is thus thought that in very early times the king of beasts was spotted like a leopard. Tiger cubs, however, are miniature likenesses of their parents from the day of their birth.

A very gorgeously tinted cat is the leopard, which is numerous throughout tropical Africa and Asia, where it frequently attacks mankind. The counterpart of this animal in our part of the world is the jaguar, which resembles it in size and form. Its spotted coat gives it camouflage or invisibility in its haunts among the leaves and branches of the forest trees on the Main.

The New World can only boast of one other species of large cat, and this is the uniformly dun-coloured puma, the most docile member of the wild-cat family. Two smaller relatives similar to the jaguar in colouring are the ocelot and the tiger-cat.

Tapir and Young.

THE TAPIR

The tapir is a curious beast, which in appearance resembles both the horse and the elephant. It is a born swimmer, but, like the hippopotamus of Africa, does not look like one. Ages ago, when the mammoth roamed the earth, the tapir was much bigger than it is now, and was widely distributed throughout the world. To-day only five species of tapir survive, and of these four inhabit the swamps of Central and South America, where they make long runs and live upon swamp and water plants.

The adult animal has a black skin, but the young is barred and spotted with white. Although a quiet animal and clumsy in appearance, it shows great agility in the water, and, like the hippo, can walk under water upon the river-bed.

This ability to swim stands it in good stead when pursued by the jaguar. But the water, too, has its terrors. The giant anaconda—the South American snake of which you read in Book III.—sometimes devours it in mid-stream, whilst the caribe or perai, the savage little fish with triangular razor-edged teeth, surrounds it in large shoals and literally tears it to pieces before it can gain the shore.

CROCODILES AND ALLIGATORS

Crocodiles and alligators would give a good account of themselves in a wild beast swimming-race. They are admirably fitted for life in the water, for besides possessing webbed feet and a tail which seems to have been specially made for propelling their bulky bodies through the water, their eyes, nostrils, and ears are situated right on the top of their heads. As a result the reptiles can use these organs when they are floating about with only the upper part of their heads exposed.

In addition to this the nostrils and ears have valves which close when the animals are submerged, thus preventing the inflow of water. Their eyes, too, are protected by transparent discs as well as eyelids, and the very broad tongue is so fixed that it forms a valve to prevent the water rushing down the throat when the mouth is open.

One often hears the question asked, "What is the difference between a crocodile and an alligator?" The differences are chiefly in the structure of these reptiles. Generally speaking, in the crocodiles the snout is more or less pointed, and the fourth tooth of the lower jaw, the largest, fits into a notch in the upper, whilst in the alligators the snout is usually rounder, and the tooth referred to fits into a pit. Crocodiles invariably remain savage in captivity, but alligators become comparatively tame.

Crocodile.

POUCHED ANIMALS

The pouched animals were some of the first of the warm-blooded, hair-bearing vertebrates to appear on earth, and many giants were amongst their ancestors. The best known of those existing to-day are the kangaroo of Australia and the manicou or opossum of South America. Others are the Tasmanian devil and the wombat.

The opossum is the only pouched animal inhabiting the New World. The young—sometimes as many as seventeen at a birth—are very weak when born, and are so helpless that they have to be transferred at once to the pouch or pocket in which they suckle, each little "possum" clinging fast to its feeding bottle.

Opossum and Young.

When old enough they leave the pouch and mount upon their mother's back, each baby taking a firm grip by its own prehensile extremity round the tail of the parent. The family, thus secured, may travel up and down the tallest of trees, over walls, or on to the roofs of houses.

The opossum is an adept at feigning death when threatened with attack.

THE ANT-EATER

The ant-eater, the sloth, and the armadillo are all more or less nocturnal animals—that is, they do most of their work at night.

The first-named inhabits the swampy forest regions of Central and South America. At first sight this animal appears to be a combination of skunk, bear, and bird. It has the tremendous tail of the skunk, the clumsy body and massive limbs of the bear, whilst its long pointed head resembles a bird's more than that of a mammal.

Ant-eater.

It is especially adapted for the destruction of ant nests and their occupants. Countless ages spent in sucking rather than chewing food have resulted in the ant-eater's lips becoming joined together until but a small opening is left, just large enough for its long whip-like tongue to pass through. There is not a sign of a tooth in its foot-long jaw-bones.

When hungry the ant-eater smashes an ant-hill with one of its powerful fore-claws. The myriads of white ants pour forth, only to be met by a long lashing tongue covered with sticky saliva. Those that adhere to it find themselves passing through that small opening and thence to the animal's interior.

The mother carries her single offspring on her back for a time. Jaguars and dogs seldom attack the ant-eater, although its flesh is good, for its hug is as deadly as that of a bear. Man, however, is fast clearing out this strange beast, although it does so much good in an ant-infested land.

Exercises

1. What does the expression "playing 'possum" mean?
2. How many animals are mentioned in this lesson? (Class names, such as reptiles, mammals, etc., not included.) Make a list of them.
3. Make sentences of your own containing these words:

   nocturnal   prehensile   appendage   receptacles
   ravaging   adhere   camouflage   miniature
   counterpart   invisibility   agility   submerged
4. What do you consider is the most interesting fact or habit described in the lesson?
5. In what ways are all members of the cat family alike?
6. How are crocodiles and alligators fitted for an aquatic life (life in the water)?
7. Fill in the blanks:
   (a) The young —— travels on its mother's ——, even among the tree-tops.
   (b) The spots on the —— and the —— render them practically invisible among the leaves of the ——.
   (c) In monkeys the —— are always longer than the ——.
   (d) The young of both the —— and the —— are spotted at first, but they —— their spots as they —— ——.
   (e) The —— gives the —— "notice to quit" when it smashes their mountain-like home with its —— paw.

THE "TEMERAIRE" TOWED TO HER LAST BERTH. (*J. M. W. Turner.*)

LESSON 12

PICTURE LESSONS—II

The Fighting Téméraire

THE painter of this picture was J. M. W. Turner, an Englishman, one of the greatest in the history of the world's art. You saw another of his pictures in Book III. He was really a poet, though he did not write poetry, for his pictures are not merely records of things seen, but are full of imagination.

He happened to be sailing down the Thames to Greenwich when the old *Téméraire* was being dragged to its last home. Being a man of imagination, the passing of the old warship stirred him to the depths, and he determined to express his feelings as well as he could in a picture. So he did what every artist is entitled to do— something, indeed, which makes him an artist and not merely a photographer—that is to say, he set this ship in a new light, and he made additions in order to express his feelings, and also to make a fine picture.

He wishes to remind us that the grand old ship is about to rest after a glorious and strenuous career. So he shows the vessel on the evening of a stormy day when the sun is sinking amidst gorgeous colours. What could be a more fitting time than this for the old warrior ship, after *its* stormy day, to pass in honour to its rest?

In fact, the picture is that of a fine procession. The stately ship passes other smaller craft on its way, but the artist brings these together in such a manner as to make them appear attendants in its retinue. He does this by composing his picture within the lines shown in the sketch below, where you see that everything is arranged so as to lead the eye from the setting sun towards the stately ship. See, too, how the black-puffing little tug becomes transformed into a kind of attendant, preceding the warrior with a flaming torch; and by its very blackness makes the old ship appear ghostly, as though passing gradually from the world of men and battles.

Even the black buoys floating near the bottom of the picture play their part, for they too not only lead the eye to one point, but they help still more to throw the old ship into the distance and add to its dignity. Moreover, the two buoys are so placed that they balance each other, and, as it were, help to keep everything *steady*, as well as to mark out the path for the slowly advancing warship.

LESSON 13

PIP AND THE CONVICT

Introduction.—This extract is the opening chapter of Dickens's novel, *Great Expectations,* which some critics have declared to contain the best of his plots. I hope it will lead you, in after years, to read the whole book. There may be a copy of it in your school library.

My father's family name being Pirrup, and my Christian name Philip, my infant tongue could make of both names nothing longer or more explicit* than Pip. So I called myself Pip, and came to be called Pip. . . .

Ours was the marsh country, down by the river, within, as the river wound, twenty miles of the sea. My first most vivid† and broad impression of the identity of things‡ seems to me to have been gained on a memorable§ raw afternoon towards evening. At such a time I found out for certain that this bleak place overgrown with nettles was the churchyard; and that Philip Pirrup, late of this parish, and also Georgiana wife of the above, were dead and buried; and that Alexander, Bartholomew, Abraham, Tobias, and Roger, infant children of the aforesaid, were also dead and buried; and that the dark flat wilderness beyond the churchyard, intersected‖ with dykes and mounds and gates, with scattered cattle feeding on it, was the marshes;

---

* Plainly stated.
† Lifelike; striking.
‡ Knowledge of what things actually were.
§ Never-to-be-forgotten.
‖ Cut across.

and that the low leaden line beyond was the river; and that the distant savage lair,* from which the wind was rushing, was the sea; and that the small bundle of shivers, growing afraid of it all and beginning to cry, was Pip.

"Hold your noise!" cried a terrible voice, as a man started up from among the graves at the side of the church porch. "Keep still, or I'll cut your throat!"

A fearful man, all in coarse grey, with a great iron on his leg. A man with no hat, and with broken shoes, and with an old rag tied round his head. A man who had been soaked in water, and smothered in mud, and lamed by stones, and cut by flints, and stung by nettles, and torn by briars; who limped and shivered, and glared† and growled; and whose teeth chattered in his head as he seized me by the chin.

"Oh! Don't cut my throat, sir," I pleaded in terror. "Pray, don't do it, sir."

"Tell us your name!" said the man. "Quick!"

"Pip, sir."

"Once more," said the man, staring at me. "Give it mouth!"

"Pip. Pip, sir."

"Show us where you live," said the man. "Pint‡ out the place!"

I pointed to where our village lay, on the flat in-shore among the alder-trees§ and pollards,‖ a mile or more from the church.

* Hiding-place of a wild animal.
† Gazed fiercely.
‡ Point.
§ Trees which grow in moist ground in temperate countries.
‖ Trees having the whole crown cut off.

The man, after looking at me for a moment, turned me upside down, and emptied my pockets. There was nothing in them but a piece of bread. When the church came to itself—for he was so sudden and strong that he made it go head over heels before me, and I saw the steeple under my feet—when the church came to itself, I say, I was seated on a high tombstone, trembling, while he ate the bread ravenously.[*] . . .

"You young dog," said he, licking his lips, "what fat cheeks you ha' got! Darn me, if I couldn't eat 'em!"

I held tighter to the tombstone on which I had been placed—partly to keep myself on it; partly to keep myself from crying.

"Now lookee here!" said the man. "Where's your mother?"

"There, sir!" said I.

He started, made a short run, and stopped and looked over his shoulder.

"There, sir!" I timidly explained. "Also Georgiana. That's my mother."

"Oh!" said he, coming back. "And is that your father alonger your mother?"

"Yes, sir," said I; "him too; late of this parish."

"Ha!" he muttered; then, considering, "Who d'ye live with—supposin' you're kindly let to live, which I han't made up my mind about?"

"My sister, sir—Mrs. Joe Gargery—wife of Joe Gargery, the blacksmith, sir."

"Blacksmith, eh?" said he. And looked down at his leg.

After darkly looking at his leg and at me several times, he came closer to my tombstone, took me by both arms, and tilted me back as far as he could hold me; so that his

---

[*] Like a hungry wild animal.

eyes looked most powerfully down into mine, and mine looked most helplessly up into his.

"He ate the bread ravenously."

"Now lookee here," he said, "the question being whether you're to be let to live. You know what a file is?"

"Yes, sir."

"And you know what wittles* is?"

"Yes, sir."

After each question he tilted me over a little more, so as to give me a greater sense of helplessness and danger.

"You get me a file." He tilted me again. "And you get me wittles." He tilted me again. "You bring 'em both to me."

* Victuals; food.

He tilted me again. "Or I'll have your heart and liver out." He tilted me again.

I was dreadfully frightened, and so giddy that I clung to him with both hands, and said, "If you would kindly please to let me keep upright, sir, perhaps I shouldn't be sick, and perhaps I could attend more."

He gave me a most tremendous dip and roll, so that the church jumped over its own weather-cock. Then he held me by the arms in an upright position on the top of the stone, and went on in these fearful terms:

"You bring me, to-morrow morning early, that file and them wittles. You bring the lot to me, at that old battery* over yonder. You do it, and you never dare to say a word or dare to make a sign concerning your having seen such a person as me, or any person sumever,† and you shall be let to live. You fail, or you go from my words in any partickler,‡ no matter how small it is, and your heart and your liver shall be tore out, roasted, and ate. I ain't alone, as you may think I am. . . . Now, what do you say?"

I said that I would get him the file, and I would get him what broken bits of food I could, and I would come to him at the battery, early in the morning.

He took me down.

"Now," he pursued,§ "you remember what you've undertook, and you get home!"

"Goo-good-night, sir," I faltered.‖

* Fort on the marshes.
† Whatsoever.
‡ Particular; small point.
§ Went on.
‖ Spoke in trembling tones.

"Much of that!" said he, glancing about him over the cold wet flat. "I wish I was a frog. Or an eel!"

At the same time he hugged his shuddering body in both his arms—clasping himself, as if to hold himself together—and limped towards the low church wall. As I saw him go, picking his way among the nettles, and among the brambles that bound the green mounds, he looked in my young eyes as if he were eluding* the hands of the dead people, stretching up cautiously out of their graves to get a twist upon his ankle and pull him in.

When he came to the low church wall, he got over it, like a man whose legs were numbed and stiff, and then turned round to look for me. When I saw him turning, I set my face towards home, and made the best use of my legs. But presently I looked over my shoulder, and saw him going on again towards the river, still hugging himself in both arms, and picking his way with his sore feet among the great stones dropped into the marshes here and there, for stepping-places when the rains were heavy or the tide was in.

The marshes were just a long black horizontal line then, as I stopped to look after him; and the river was just another horizontal line, not nearly so broad nor yet so black; and the sky was just a row of long angry red lines and dense black lines intermixed.

On the edge of the river I could faintly make out the only two black things in all the prospect† that seemed to be standing upright: one of these was the beacon by which the sailors steered—like an unhooped cask upon a

---

* Getting out of the way of by means of a trick.
† Stretch of country that I could see.

pole—an ugly thing when you were near it; the other a gibbet,* with some chains hanging to it which had once held a pirate. The man was limping on towards this latter, as if he were the pirate come to life, and come down, and going back to hook himself up again. It gave me a terrible turn when I thought so; and as I saw the cattle lifting their heads to gaze after him, I wondered whether they thought so too. But now I was frightened again, and ran home without stopping.

EXERCISES

1. How did Pip get his name?
2. Describe the picture on page 79.
3. The convict did not speak correct English. Make a list of all the corrections you find necessary in his grammar and spelling.
4. Describe in your own words the country round Pip's home.
5. Make sentences containing the following words:

Expectations,	memorable,	timidly,	horizontal,
critics,	intersected,	tremendous,	prospect,
explicit,	dykes,	pursued,	gibbet,
vivid,	lair,	faltered,	pirate.
impression,	glared,	eluding,	
identity,	ravenously,	cautiously,	

6. Write out and learn the following "golden rule" of Charles Dickens: "Whatever I have tried to do in life, I have tried with all my heart to do well. What I have devoted myself to, I have devoted myself to completely. Never to put one hand to anything on which I could throw my whole self, I find now to have been my golden rule."

* Gallows.

LESSON 14

THE LIVING PLANT—II

LEAVES

LEAVES are to plants what lungs are to human beings, as they are the chief organs through which the plant breathes. They also manufacture food for its use and give off excess water taken up by the roots.

The varieties of leaves are so numerous, that if you were to collect a number from different kinds of plants it would be a very difficult matter to find two exactly alike. Most leaves, however, are composed of a stalk and a blade, and they grow from joints in the stem, but at varying distances according to the kind of plant. The leaves are arranged on the stem in such a way as to allow each to get as much light as possible. The stalk also serves to spread them out to the light to better advantage, and it acts as a conductor of food just as the stem does.

The blade of the leaf, besides varying in shape, also varies in texture from a leathery substance to one resembling paper. The tissue of the leaf is supported by a system of veins of various patterns; sometimes there is a well-marked midrib, with numerous branches connected by a network of veins, as in the bean; in other cases, as in corn, the veins run parallel to each other and do not form a network. You can see the forms of the veins in the drawings on the next page.

If you examine the surfaces of different kinds of leaves, you will find that some are so thickly covered with

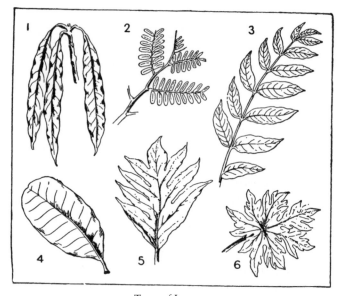

Types of Leaves.
1. Mango. 2. Tamarind. 3. Cedar. 4. Cashew. 5. Breadfruit. 6. Papaw.

hairs that they feel like velvet, some have few hairs, whilst others are quite smooth. Prickles or spines which serve as a protection to the plant are also found on certain leaves. Sometimes, as in the case of peas, the leaves or parts of them form tendrils, by which the climbing stems are supported and the plant pulled up to obtain its air and sunshine.

In Part I. of this lesson it was shown that water is absorbed by the root hairs, and taken through the main roots and stems to the leaves of the plant. This water contains the various food substances in solution. You can observe the movement of water throughout the plant by putting freshly cut stems of shiny bush into water coloured red with red ink, when after a short time a pink colour will be noticed spreading through the stem and leaves.

During daylight plants give off large quantities of surplus water, chiefly through minute openings, or little mouths, usually on the under-sides of the leaves. This does not take place in the dark, as the little openings in the leaves are then closed.

This process of giving off water is known as *transpiration*. The water lost through the leaves is replaced by a fresh supply drawn up through the roots and stems. You can see, therefore, that it is of great importance that plants should obtain sufficient water to make up for that given off, or the leaves will droop and wither.

The stronger the sunshine, and the more windy and warm the weather, the greater is the evaporation of water, as we learnt in Book II., so that with our steady "trade wind" breezes and our warm tropical sunshine, evaporation is greater in our countries than in those of the temperate zone. Hence the water given off by plants quickly disappears into the atmosphere.

It is a common sight in the West Indies to see the leaves of plants become limp during the heat of the day, yet regain their firmness when the sun goes down. Why is this?

Plants have many devices to prevent excessive transpiration, and also to counteract the effect of the dry season, when they obtain little moisture from the soil. In your Nature Study lessons you will doubtless learn about these wonderful means which Nature has provided.

Besides giving off water, leaves also send out a gas known as oxygen, and absorb another gas from the air, called carbon dioxide. This gas is split up into its parts, the oxygen being set free and the carbon retained by the plant. This carbon, together with the water and mineral salts taken up by the roots, is converted in the leaves into food material of the nature of sugars and starches suitable for the growth of the plant. This manufacture of plant food can only take place in the green parts of plants and during daylight. It is known as *assimilation.*

There is a third process carried on by plants, not only in the leaves, but also in other growing parts. This process is called *respiration,* and is very similar to the breathing of animals, as oxygen gas is absorbed from the atmosphere and carbon dioxide given off. Respiration is always going on, but assimilation only occurs under the conditions described in the previous paragraph.

A very important, but often overlooked, use of leaves is to distribute, in the directions where the plant most needs it, the water which falls on them as rain. They do this by means of their position and arrangement on the plant. We have seen that roots take in their food through the fine hairs on the young rootlets, so that the water is required at that part of the soil where these rootlets are to be found. Study some young plants, such as tobacco, cabbage, and beet, to see how the leaves send the rain water towards the centre of the plant. Then look at older plants whose roots have gone farther afield, and notice the different ways the leaves bend. Where is the water required by a large tree? Near the trunk or some distance away? What do the leaves do in this case?

Flowers

Most plants produce flowers at some period of their life history. Flowers vary considerably in appearance; some are large and showy, whereas others are difficult to see, being small and inconspicuous; some are sweetly scented, whilst others have practically no smell.

Cacao Tree, showing Flowers and Fruit at the same time.
(*Photo: Messrs. Cadbury.*)

They also vary very much in their general form and the manner in which they are borne on the plant. Some grow in clusters, as in the various kinds of cassias, forming what is known as an *inflorescence*, and others grow singly, as in the guava. They may have stalks—either short or long—or be entirely without them.

Flowers are usually borne on the younger parts of plants, but in some instances, such as the cacao, the cannon-ball tree, and the calabash, we find them even on the old trunks and branches. Some grow at the tops of the plants, whilst others arise on the stems from near the base of the leaf-stalk.

Each individual flower is made up of separate members, having their own different functions to perform; occasionally some of these parts may be absent, just as we saw was the case with the entire plant. When this is so, the missing members are either borne on other flowers, as in the pumpkin, or other parts may take on their special work.

The members or parts of a flower are the *sepals,* the *petals,* the *stamens,* the *pistil,* and the *ovary.*

In order to recognize and to understand the use of these parts thoroughly, we will take a flower of the guava tree and pull it to pieces.* On the outside we find four green sepals, bent backwards towards the stalk. When the flower was still in the bud stage these sepals quite enveloped the other parts of the flower, forming a protective covering to them.

Within the sepals and next to them are the white petals. These are opposite the gaps between the sepals, and are also bent backwards. Petals are usually conspicuously coloured (in this case white) so as to attract insects. In some flowers which have no petals, the sepals are coloured instead; and in others, such as lilies, both are coloured.

The cluster of white threads within the petals are the stamens, at the tips of which are the little bodies, called anthers, which bear the pollen.

---

* *Note to Teacher.*—This should be done in conjunction with the reading, and the substance of the lesson will then be more easily understood.

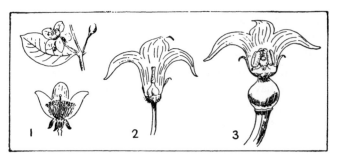

1. Guava Flower and Section.   2, 3. Male and Female Pumpkin
Flowers.

In the centre of the flower is the pistil, which stands erect and is stouter than the stamens. At its base you will find the ovary, which is the somewhat egg-shaped structure just below the sepals. The ovary will later develop into the guava fruit if the tiny grains of pollen from the stamens are transferred by wind, insects, or any other agency to the stick or tip of the pistil.

After reaching the tip the pollen grains germinate or grow, and grow right down through the pistil and fertilize the little bodies called the ovules, which are lying in the ovary. These will then grow and develop into seeds. This entrance of the pollen grains into the ovules or undeveloped seeds in the ovary is known as *fertilization,* because the seeds then become *fertile,* or able to produce other plants of their kind, when subjected to conditions in which they will germinate.

The process of transferring the pollen from the stamens to the pistil is known as *pollination.* Flowers which are pollinated by wind are usually less conspicuous, and bear more pollen than those which are pollinated by insects.

The latter are usually attractive in colour and scent, and contain honey.

If you examine the flowers of the pumpkin you will find that they are not all alike. All have sepals and petals, but some have stamens and no pistil, others a pistil and no stamens. The pollen has to be carried from the stamens of one flower to the pistil of another, and the young pumpkin will then grow from the pistil. The pollen is usually transferred by insects which visit flowers of this kind in search of honey.

Such insects come into contact with the stamens, and some of the pollen adheres to them. When they visit another flower which has a pistil, some of these grains are deposited upon it. In this way bees, butterflies, moths, and also humming birds, carry on the work of pollination. Man can also pollinate flowers by shaking pollen on to the pistil.

Flowers are usually the chief means by which botanists classify plants into different families, such as the orchid family, the hibiscus family, and the lily family. On looking at flowers belonging to each of these families, although you will readily observe differences of detail, you will have no difficulty in recognizing a general resemblance.

EXERCISES

1. Explain the difference between "born" and "borne." Use each of these words in sentences of your own to show you understand their meaning.
2. In this lesson you have learned of several processes which take place in the living plant. State briefly what each of the following processes consists of: Transpiration, assimilation, respiration, pollination, fertilization.
3. Make drawings of the following leaves: Mango, papaw, cashew, cedar, tamarind, and breadfruit.

4. In what way or ways is a plant like an animal? How does it differ from an animal?

5. Why do the leaves of the sugar-cane bend outwards and downwards at the tops, while they still incline inwards at the base?

6. What are the parts of a flower? What work does each part perform? Illustrate your answer by a drawing.

7. Explain in what ways insects assist the living plant.

8. Fill in the blanks:

   (a) In the flowers of the pumpkin that which has the —— is the male flower, whereas the one with the pistil is the —— flower.

   (b) The tiny —— are on the —— surface of the leaf. Although they are like little —— they are not used for eating purposes, but only for —— air in and ——, and giving out ——.

   (c) The leaves —— the food for the —— plant. They make it from the —— and the —— supplied by the ——.

   (d) The banana has the power of —— the position of its leaves, so that the sunlight —— less directly on ——. This lessens the ——.

9. Make a list of the uses of leaves to the plant.

LESSON 15

ADMIRAL VERNON

A MAN of a different type from Benbow was Admiral Vernon, though, like Benbow, Vernon also in his day was extremely popular; for did not he with six ships storm and take a great city on the Main, before which, fourteen years earlier, a British fleet of twenty line-of-battle ships— through the fault of the Government and not of the admiral in command—rotted in inaction, losing more than

"FORCED AN ENTRANCE THROUGH THE EMBRASURES." (*See page 96.*)

three thousand officers and men by disease, for fighting there was none?

Unlike Benbow, Vernon was a man of ancient family, as his ancestors received lands from William the Conqueror in 1066; his father was a Secretary of State or one of the King's Ministers.

Born in 1684, Edward Vernon was educated at one of the best schools in England, where, from his love of the sea, he was nicknamed "the Admiral." Later he went to Oxford University, from which he seems to have entered the navy at about the age of seventeen. At twenty-two he was a post-captain, and in 1708, in command of the *Jersey* (48 guns), he came to the West Indies, one of our numerous struggles with France being then in progress. Until 1713, when a treaty of peace was signed, he continued to distinguish himself, capturing many of the enemy's vessels.

By the year 1722 Vernon had entered Parliament, where he endeavoured to stiffen up the policy of the Government in their dealings with Spain in the West Indies. He was willing to forfeit reputation and life, he said on one occasion, if with no greater force than half a dozen ships of the line he could not undertake to capture Porto Bello (which was then, excepting Havana and Cartagena, the most formidable stronghold in this part of the world, and which you will remember was once stormed by Morgan the Buccaneer). The Government jumped at his offer, and in July 1739 Vernon was appointed Admiral and Commander-in-Chief of His Majesty's ships in the West Indies.

Raw, untrained, inexperienced landsmen formed the bulk of the crews of the vessels ordered by Government to serve under Vernon's orders in this expedition. But the admiral was not of the stuff to let himself be discouraged or dismayed. A strong protest was indeed sent to Government, but he sturdily set himself to the task of making his men fit for their work, and by the time Jamaica was reached the landlubbers had been transformed into smart seamen, ready for anything.

On the 5th of November 1739 the squadron sailed from Port Royal for Porto Bello. The whole force consisted of the *Burford* (70 guns), Vernon's flagship, the *Hampton Court* (70), *Worcester* (60), *Stafford* (60), *Princess Louisa* (60), *Norwich* (50), and a frigate.

Porto Bello, a place of great strength protected by three formidable forts, was considered by the Spaniards to be all but impregnable; in any case its capture would be a task far beyond the power of a small squadron such as that commanded by Vernon. Strong, indeed, it was, but, perhaps for that very reason—as in the case of Gibraltar in 1704— the Spaniards had been slipshod in their preparations. But if they trusted confidently in the strength of its walls, they did not know Vernon; nor did they know the spirit of the men he commanded.

Of the three forts guarding the bay of Porto Bello, the two most formidable, Castel del Ferro and Gloria Castle, stood at the entrance, one on either headland; nearer the town was San Geronymo. It was Admiral Vernon's plan that the two leading ships should pass within a cable's length of Castel del Ferro, "giving the enemy as they pass as warm a fire as possible both from great guns and musketry," then to steer for Gloria Castle, where they were to anchor as near the fort as the water would allow them to come, and from that position to batter down the defences. The third ship, after discharging a broadside at the Castel del Ferro, was to head for San Geronymo, there to anchor and batter its works, whilst the admiral and the two remaining vessels of the squadron would anchor abreast of Castel del Ferro and smother it with their fire.

On arrival off Porto Bello the wind was so light as almost to deprive the vessels of steerage-way, and they therefore anchored some miles off shore. Neither did the wind serve the admiral's plans next morning, and it was not possible to carry out the attack as originally ordered. Instead, owing to a sudden failure of the breeze that was taking them in, the whole force of the squadron was concentrated on Castel del Ferro.

The *Hampton Court,* as she swept slowly past in the lead, opened a furious cannonade on the castle, firing no less than four hundred rounds from her big guns in the first twenty-five minutes; and the other ships, as they came up, joining in, brought such a weight of metal to bear on the walls that soon the Spaniards were seen deserting their guns. Then from the flagship fluttered out the signal to land, and a crowd of boats dashed for the shore, the ships keeping up meanwhile a heavy fire to cover the landing-party.

The Spaniards in the lower battery of the castle still worked their guns, however; the walls were quite unbreached, and no scaling-ladders were available. A few of Vernon's men had already fallen, and a land force might have been sorely put to it to make further progress; but the places are few which a British sailor cannot get into, or out of, when he has a mind. There were no scaling-ladders, indeed, but the men made ladders of themselves, and scrambling over each other's shoulders, forced an entrance through the embrasures under the mouths of the lower battery guns, hauled up the marines, and speedily made themselves masters of that work.

The garrison of the castle surrendered, and next day, without further fighting, Castle Gloria and Fort San Geronymo hauled down their flags and capitulated, together with several men-of-war then lying in the harbour. The loss sustained by the squadron was astonishingly small, not exceeding twenty killed and wounded. No great plunder was taken—times were not as in the days of the old buccaneers—but ten thousand dollars, which had arrived from Spain a few days before for the pay of the garrison of Porto Bello, were distributed amongst the British ships, to the no small content of the men, as appears from the letter of one of the sailors, which stated: "Our dear admiral ordered every man some Spanish dollars to be immediately given, which is like a man of honour."

The enthusiasm in England over this victory was immense; medals were struck in Vernon's honour, songs were written of which he was the hero, the freedom of the City of London was presented to him, and he received the thanks of both Houses of Parliament.

. . . . . .

After refitting at Port Royal, Admiral Vernon treated Cartagena to a three days' bombardment, but, though he severely damaged its fortifications, the force at his disposal was not strong enough to enable him to attempt the capture of the town.

Fired by Vernon's great success, the British Government now decided to send out a powerful force, wherewith the Admiral was instructed to harass Spain in the West Indies, and to attack her principal settlements. When the new fleet left Port Royal it consisted of no fewer than thirty-one line-of-battle ships, a force with which Vernon might reasonably consider himself capable of overpowering any possible opposition. If with his small squadron of six ships he had already accomplished so much, what might he not hope to do with the magnificent force now at his disposal, especially as work on shore would now no longer be hampered by lack of troops? With the fleet had arrived from England transports carrying ten thousand troops. Yet it was just this very circumstance, the presence of the troops, that proved Vernon's undoing.

The land forces were under the command of General Wentworth, an officer totally unfitted for such a post, being timid and wavering, and without self-reliance or sufficient experience. As long as the work was confined to the ships and the seamen, all went well; but when Wentworth's authority in connection with the land operations began to be exercised, then disaster commenced. Like Penn and Venables in Jamaica nearly one hundred years earlier, Vernon and Wentworth could not pull together, and although they made several attempts to wrest from Spain some of her land possessions, little success attended their efforts. We find in consequence that even to-day Britain has no foothold in the lands in Central and South America that were known in those days as the Spanish Main.

EXERCISES

1. Draw a map of the harbour of Porto Bello from the information given in this lesson. Indicate the positions of the forts.
2. Imagine you were the sailor who wrote the letter quoted. Write the whole letter as he would have written it to his wife.
3. In what ways was Vernon like Benbow, and in what was he of a different type?
4. British Honduras and British Guiana (now known as Belize and Guyana) were the only British possessions on the mainland of Central and South America. How can you explain the absence of more British colonies in that area?
5. Study the picture on page 92. The men in red coats are the marines. What was their special work? What other men can you see?
6. Explain why the capture of Porto Bello is considered one of the most remarkable exploits in the annals of the British navy.
7. Find Porto Bello on the map. Describe its exact position. How many miles is it in a straight line from Port Royal (now Kingston)? How is its name now spelt?

LESSON 16

THE BURIAL OF SIR JOHN MOORE

Introduction.—In the early years of the nineteenth century there was a prolonged struggle between England and France, which culminated in the battle of Waterloo in 1815. Previous to this an English army, commanded by Sir John Moore, was compelled to retreat to the coast at Corunna, in the northwest of Spain, through 250 miles of difficult country in midwinter, pursued by the French forces under Soult. Corunna was reached on January 13, 1809, and three days later, the transports having arrived, the embarkation was proceeding when the French army came in sight and immediately attacked.

In the engagement Moore was struck by a grape-shot which shattered his shoulder. He was carried into the town, where he died after hearing of the defeat of the French. He was buried in the citadel at dawn the following day, just as the French artillery opened fire, and the army at once sailed for England. The French guns paid him funeral honours, and the Spanish commander, the Marquis de la Romana, erected a monument over his grave.

This solemn, dignified poem describing his funeral was written by an Irish clergyman, Charles Wolfe, who died in 1823. Although he wrote other poems, this is the only one that is remembered; it is sure to live for ever.

West Indians will be interested to know that Sir John Moore had survived a severe attack of fever in St. Lucia before he assumed command of the British forces in the Peninsula.

NOT a drum was heard, not a funeral note,
　　As his corse to the rampart we hurried;
Not a soldier discharged his farewell shot
　　O'er the grave where our hero we buried.

We buried him darkly at dead of night,
　　The sods with our bayonets turning,
By the struggling moonbeam's misty light
　　And the lanthorn dimly burning.

No useless coffin enclosed his breast,
　　Not in sheet or in shroud we wound him;
But he lay like a warrior taking his rest,
　　With his martial cloak around him.

Few and short were, the prayers we said,
　　And we spoke not a word of sorrow;
But we steadfastly gazed on the face that was dead,
　　And we bitterly thought of the morrow.

We thought, as we hollowed his narrow bed
　　And smoothed down his lonely pillow,
That the foe and the stranger would tread o'er his head
　　And we far away on the billow!

Lightly they'll talk of the spirit that's gone,
    And o'er his cold ashes upbraid him—
But little hell reck, if they let him sleep on
    In the grave where a Briton has laid him.

But half of our heavy task was done
    When the clock struck the hour for retiring;
And we heard the distant and random gun
    That the foe was sullenly firing.

Slowly and sadly we laid him down,
    From the field of his fame fresh and gory;
We carved not a line, and we raised not a stone,
    But we left him alone with his glory.

                          CHARLES WOLFE.

EXERCISES

1. The introduction tells you something of the history of the events; but remember that there is something better than historical facts in this poem. What do you think it is?
2. Study the language of the verses. Is the meaning always clear? Are the lines smooth-sounding or rough?
3. Is the poem serious, sad, melancholy, miserable, gloomy, hopeless, inspiring, proud, dignified, savage, noble, or grave? Or is it more than one of these things?
4. Study the phrases. Which do you like best?
5. Why is this a good poem for reading aloud?
6. Does the poem suggest a picture? If so, indicate roughly how it ought to be composed.
7. There is character in words, which can be discovered if we linger over them—such words as home, brother, glory, sorrow, warrior, love, joy, peace, hope. What other words appeal to you?
8. Find Corunna on the map.
9. Give the date of the battle of Corunna.

LESSON 17

THE PRAYING MANTIS

I.—Her Hunting

THERE is an insect of the south that is quite as interesting as the cicada,* but much less famous, because it makes no noise. Had it been provided with cymbals, its renown would have been greater than the celebrated musician's, for it is most unusual both in shape and habits.

The Praying Mantis.

A long time ago, in the days of ancient Greece, this insect was named mantis, or the prophet. The peasant saw her on the sun-scorched grass, standing half-erect in a very imposing and majestic manner, with her broad green gossamer wings trailing like long veils, and her fore-legs, like arms, raised to the sky as though in prayer. To the peasant's ignorance the insect seemed like a priestess or a nun, and so she came to be called the praying mantis.

There was never a greater mistake! Those pious airs are a fraud; those arms raised in prayer are really the most

---

* The *cicada* is an insect remarkable for its chirping sound, made by a kind of cymbal in a cavity behind its wings.

horrible weapons, which slay whatever passes within reach. The mantis is fierce as a tigress, cruel as an ogress. She feeds only on living creatures.

There is nothing in her appearance to inspire dread. She is not without a certain beauty, with her slender, graceful figure, her pale-green colouring, and her long gauze wings. Having a flexible neck, she can move her head freely in all directions. She is the only insect that can direct her gaze wherever she will. She almost has a face.

Great is the contrast between this peaceful-looking body and the murderous machinery of the fore-legs. The haunch is very long and powerful, while the thigh is even longer, and carries on its lower surface two rows of sharp spikes or teeth. Behind these teeth are three spurs. In short, the thigh is a saw with two blades, between which the leg lies when folded back.

This leg itself is also a double-edged saw, provided with a greater number of teeth than the thigh. It ends in a strong hook with a point as sharp as a needle, and a double blade like a curved pruning-knife. I have many painful memories of this hook. Many a time, when mantis-hunting, I have been clawed by the insect and forced to ask somebody else to release me. No insect in this part of the world[*] is so troublesome to handle. The mantis claws you with her pruning-hooks, pricks you with her spikes, seizes you in her vice, and makes self-defence impossible if you wish to keep your captive alive.

When at rest, the trap is folded back against the chest and looks quite harmless. There you have the insect

---

[*] The south of Europe.

praying. But if a victim passes by, the appearance of prayer is quickly dropped. The three long divisions of the trap are suddenly unfolded, and the prey is caught with the sharp hook at the end of them, and drawn back between the two saws. Then the vice closes, and all is over. Locusts, grasshoppers, and even stronger insects are helpless against the four rows of teeth.

It is impossible to make a complete study of the habits of the mantis in the open fields, so I am obliged to take her indoors. She can live quite happily in a pan filled with sand and covered with a gauze dish-cover, if only she be supplied with plenty of fresh food. In order to find out what can be done by the strength and daring of the mantis, I provide her not only with locusts and grasshoppers, but also with the largest spiders of the neighbourhood. This is what I see.

A grey locust, heedless of danger, walks towards the mantis. The latter gives a convulsive shiver, and suddenly, in the most surprising way, strikes an attitude that fills the locust with terror. The wing-covers open; the wings spread to their full extent and stand erect like sails, towering over the insect's back; the tip of the body curls up like a crook, rising and falling with short jerks, and making a sound like the puffing of a startled adder. Planted defiantly on its four hind-legs, the mantis holds the front part of its body almost upright. The murderous legs open wide, and show a pattern of black-and-white spots beneath them.

In this strange attitude the mantis stands motionless, with eyes fixed on her prey. If the locust moves the mantis turns her head. The object of this performance is plain. It is intended to strike terror into the heart of the victim, to paralyse it with fright before attacking it. The mantis is pretending to be a ghost!

The plan is quite successful. The locust sees a spectre before him, and gazes at it without moving. He to whom leaping is so easy makes no attempt at escape. He stays stupidly where he is, or even draws nearer with a leisurely step. As soon as he is within reach of the mantis she strikes with her claws; her double saws close and clutch; the poor wretch protests in vain; the cruel ogress begins her meal.

The pretty crab spider stabs her victim in the neck, in order to poison it and make it helpless. In the same way the mantis attacks the locust first at the back of the neck, to destroy its power of movement. This enables her to kill and eat an insect as big as herself, or even bigger. It is amazing that the greedy creature can contain so much food.

The various digger-wasps receive visits from her pretty frequently. Posted near the burrows on a liane, she waits for a chance to bring near her a double prize, the hunting-wasp and the prey she is bringing home. The wasp is suspicious and on her guard: still, now and then a rash one is caught. With a sudden rustle of wings the mantis terrifies the newcomer, who hesitates for a moment in her fright. Then, with the sharpness of a spring, the wasp is fixed as in a trap between the blades of the double saw. The victim is then gnawed in small mouthfuls.

I once saw a bee-eating wasp, while carrying a bee to her storehouse, attacked and caught by a mantis. The wasp was in the act of eating the honey she had found in the bee's crop. The double saw of the mantis closed suddenly on the feasting wasp; but neither terror nor torture could persuade that greedy creature to leave off eating. Even while she was herself being actually devoured she continued to lick the honey from her bee!

I regret to say that, the meals of this savage ogress are not confined to other kinds of insects. For all her sanctimonious airs she is a cannibal. She will eat her sister as calmly as she would eat a grasshopper; and those around her will make no protest, being quite ready to do the same on the first opportunity. Indeed, she even makes a habit of devouring her mate.

She is worse than the wolf; for it is said that even wolves never eat each other.

II.—HER NEST

After all, however, the mantis has her good points like most people. She makes a most marvellous nest.

This nest is to be found more or less everywhere in sunny places: on stones, wood, twigs, or dry grass, and even on such things as bits of brick, strips of linen, or the shrivelled leather of an old boot. Any support will serve, as long as there is an uneven surface to form a solid foundation.

In size the nest is between one and two inches long, and less than an inch wide; and its colour is as golden as a grain of corn. It is made of a frothy substance, which has become solid and hard, and it smells like silk when it is burnt. The shape of it varies according to the support on which it is based, but in all cases the upper surface is convex. One can distinguish three bands, or zones, of which the middle one is made of little plates or scales, arranged in pairs and overlapping like the tiles of a roof. The edges of these plates are free, forming two rows of slits or little doorways, through which the young mantis escapes at the moment of hatching. In every other part the wall of the nest is impenetrable.

The eggs are arranged in layers, with the ends containing the heads pointed towards the doorways. Of these doorways, as I have just said, there are two rows. One half of the grubs will go out through the right door, and the other half through the left.

It is a remarkable fact that the mother mantis builds this cleverly-made nest while she is actually laying her eggs. From her body she produces a sticky substance rather like the caterpillar's silk-fluid; and this material she mixes with the air and whips into froth. She beats it into foam with two ladles that she has at the tip of her body, just as we beat white of egg with a fork. The foam is greyish-white, almost like soapsuds, and when it first appears it is sticky; but two minutes afterwards it has solidified.

In this sea of foam the mantis deposits her eggs. As each layer of eggs is laid, it is covered with froth, which quickly becomes solid.

As soon as she has done her work the mother withdraws. I expected to see her return and show some tender feeling for the cradle of her family, but it evidently has no further interest for her.

The mantis, I fear, has no heart. She eats her husband, and deserts her children.

III.—THE HATCHING OF HER EGGS

The eggs of the mantis usually hatch in bright sunshine, at about ten o'clock on a mid-June morning.

As I have already told you, there is only one part of the nest where the grub can find an outlet, namely, the band of scales round the middle. From under each of these scales one sees slowly appearing a blunt, transparent lump, followed by two large black specks, which are the creature's eyes. The baby grub slips gently under the thin plate and half releases itself. It is reddish yellow, and has a thick, swollen head. Under its outer skin it is quite easy to distinguish the large black eyes, the mouth flattened against the chest, the legs plastered to the body from front to back.

The young mantis finds it necessary to wear an overall when it is coming into the world, for the sake of convenience and safety. It has to emerge from the depths of the nest through narrow, winding ways, in which full-spread slender limbs could not find enough room. The creature therefore appears in swaddling-clothes, in the shape of a boat, from which it frees itself very soon.

It is a striking sight to see a hundred young mantes coming from the nest at once. Hardly does one tiny creature show its black eyes under a scale before a swarm of others appears. It is as though a signal passed from one to the other, so swiftly does the hatching spread. Almost in a moment the middle zone of the nest is covered with grubs, who run about feverishly, stripping themselves of their torn garments. Then they drop off, or clamber into the nearest foliage. A few days later a fresh swarm appears, and so on till all the eggs are hatched.

But alas! the poor grubs are hatched into a world of dangers. The ants, above all, are their enemies. They seldom succeed in entering the nest; its walls form too strong a fortress. But they wait outside for their prey.

The moment the young grubs appear they are grabbed by the ants, pulled out of their sheaths, and cut in pieces. You see piteous struggles between the little creatures who can only protest with wild wrigglings and the ferocious brigands who are carrying them off. In a moment the massacre is over; all that is left of the flourishing family is a few scattered survivors who have escaped by accident.

It is curious that the mantis, the scourge of the insect race, should be herself so often devoured at this early stage of her life by one of the least of that race, the ant. But this does not continue long. So soon as she has become firm and strong from contact with the air the mantis can hold her own. She trots about briskly among the ants, who fall back as she passes, no longer daring to tackle her.

But the mantis has another enemy who is less easily dismayed. The little grey lizard, the lover of sunny walls, pays small heed to threatening attitudes. With the tip of his slender tongue he picks up, one by one, the few stray insects that have escaped the ant. They make but a small mouthful, but to judge from the lizard's expression they taste very good. Every time he gulps down one of the little creatures he half-closes his eyelids, a sign of profound satisfaction.

The mantis lays, perhaps, a thousand eggs. Possibly only one couple of these escapes destruction.

JEAN HENRI FABRE.
From *Fabre's Book of Insects*.

Exercises

1. How did the praying mantis get its name?
2. Make a list of all the insects named in this lesson. Which do you know, and which are unfamiliar to you?
3. Examine the praying mantis in your school Nature Study collection. Compare its legs with the description given in Part I. Draw the mantis.
4. Complete the following:
   (a) As *tiger* is to *tigress*, so is —— to *ogress*.
   (b) As *ant* is to *ants*, so is *mantis* to ——.
5. Show which are the good points and which the bad points about the praying mantis.
6. The female lays a thousand eggs, and yet the insect is not very commonly seen. Why is this? What are its enemies?
7. What words in the lesson have a similar meaning to the following?

consumed	still	substance
reverent	pauses	stuck
fear	shrunk	frail
shake	basis	clothes

8. Which do you consider is the most interesting fact you have learned about this wonderful creature?

LESSON 18

PICTURE LESSONS—III

Joan of Arc

INGRES, the French artist who painted this picture, is one of the most celebrated in the world for his clever and exact drawing. We shall see later that though some artists, such as the French painter Millet, drew in a very different style, without such close exactness, they were not less notable or less true to nature.

JOAN OF ARC AT THE CONSECRATION OF CHARLES VII.
(*Ingres.*)

Ingres was a man who, as it were, saw and drew every petal or every detail, even to the pattern on a robe or the stitching on a cloth; yet he did not lose the dignity of the whole subject.

This picture shows Joan of Arc at the moment when she has reached the end of her triumphant struggles with the invading English, and has accompanied Charles VII., the French king, to the cathedral of Rheims for his consecration after victory. The artist shows Joan standing as attendant to the king, though her eyes and thoughts are turned heavenward in thankfulness for the angelic help, which, she believed, was always granted to her in battle.

Now, in composing such a picture, in which the main figure is so much larger than the others, and in which it takes up the greater part of the space, the artist has not the same difficulties to deal with as Millais had in his painting of "Raleigh's Boyhood"; but it is, at the same time, not easy to add other figures so as to avoid interfering with the main figure, or belittling it. In fact, all such additions should assist in bringing out that principal figure and its significance more clearly.

So Ingres has placed Joan exactly in the middle of the picture, and to give additional dignity, he has put in many straight lines, such as the pillars in the background, the edges of the altar and the objects on it, and, above all, the red staff that Joan holds in her right hand. The banner hanging from this staff draws attention to the king, who is only half seen, yet must be brought into the picture, though he is, for the moment, less important than Joan in the eyes of all.

The kneeling priest bends in such a way as to lead the eye from himself to the head of Joan; and the pages behind raise their hands with the like result. Further, in composing the picture the artist has not only made use of these parts to add dignity to his work, but he has brought Joan into strong relief by placing the upper portion of her figure before a dark awning or canopy.

LESSON 19

IVANHOE

Introduction.—The following extracts are taken from *Ivanhoe*, Sir Walter Scott's famous novel, dealing with the same period as *The Talisman*, of which we read in Book IV, After reading this lesson you will probably want to follow the fortunes of the Disinherited Knight still further. You can do so by reading the book.

I.—THE TOURNAMENT

THE tournament was to be held a mile out of the town of Ashby, in a beautiful green meadow, which looked as if it had been made for that very purpose. There was a perfectly flat space of turf, a quarter of a mile long, where the sports were to take place, and all round this flat space the ground sloped upwards, so that the sightseers from the higher ground could see everything quite comfortably. Galleries had been erected here for nobles and their ladies, and spread with carpets and furnished with cushions.

At one end of the flat space of ground was a platform, and on the platform were pitched five magnificent pavilions, decorated with flags of red and black, which were the chosen colours of the five knights challengers; the shield of each knight hung in front of his pavilion.

The pavilion in the middle, as the place of honour, had been given to Brian de Bois-Guilbert, who had been chosen as their leader by the other challengers.

On one side of his tent were pitched the pavilions of Reginald Front-de-Bœuf and Richard de Malvoisin, and on the other side were those of Hugh de Grantemesnil and Ralph de Vipont. And these four knights, with Brian de Bois-Guilbert, made up the five challengers who were ready to fight with all those who dared to answer their challenge.

Prince John (the brother of Richard Lion Heart) rode with his train of knights up and down the lists—the flat space where the sports were to take place—looking up at the richly dressed nobles in the galleries and the beautifully dressed ladies, speaking to one here, or shouting joyously to another there, or waving his hand to the great crowd gathered on the sloping sides above the galleries, till a marshal cried out:

"Let the prince take his seat. The time advances, and the sports should now begin."

John then dismounted, and took his seat on the throne, and called to the heralds, "Make known the laws of the tournament!"

So the heralds cried out that, firstly, the five challengers would undertake all comers.

Secondly, that any knight wishing to fight, might, if he pleased, select any one of the challengers by touching his shield.

Thirdly, that when the challengers had each taken five lances, Prince John would declare the victor of the first day's tournament; and that the victor would receive for his prize a beautiful war-horse of matchless strength; and that he should be allowed to choose the lady who took his fancy most as the Queen of Love and Beauty.

The heralds then withdrew, and none were left in the lists save the marshals of the field, who sat on horseback as still as statues.

Now in an enclosed space just outside the lists, there was a large number of knights waiting to prove their skill against the five challengers. Of these, five were chosen by lot. Then the barriers were opened, and these five knights advanced slowly into the lists.

Steadily they advanced up the sloping alley to the platform upon which the tents of the challengers stood, and, separating themselves, each touched, with the reverse of his lance, the shield of the challenger with whom he wished to fight; and then they went back to the very end of the lists, where they remained drawn up in a line.

Now the law of the sport was that if a knight touched the challenger's shield with the *reverse* of his lance they would fight merely for the sport of the game, and a piece of round, flat board was fixed on the end of the lance, so that no one need be cut or injured. But if the shield was touched with the *sharp* end of the lance, the knights would fight with sharp weapons as in real battle.

And now the challengers, each coming out of his own pavilion, mounted their horses, and, headed by Brian de Bois-Guilbert, stood opposite to the knights who had touched their shields. At the flourish of trumpets, they started out against each other at full gallop, and soon the four unlucky knights who had touched the shields of Bois-Guilbert, Front-de-Bœuf, Malvoisin, and Grantmesnil were rolling on the ground.

The fifth knight alone upheld the honour of his party, for he and Ralph de Vipont both splintered their lances without advantage on either side.

The trumpets blared. The multitude shouted. The heralds proclaimed that the challengers were victors. The challengers retreated to their pavilions triumphant. And the unfortunate knights, picking themselves up as well as they could, withdrew from the lists in shame and disgrace.

A second party, and after that a third party of knights took the field, yet the victory always remained with the challengers; for not one of them even lost his seat. At the fourth trial only three knights appeared, and these took care not to touch the shields of Brian de Bois-Guilbert or Front-de-Bœuf, who were seen to be the strongest there. But they, too, met with the same fate, and were soon rolled over by the other challengers.

Then there was a long pause. No other knights seemed to be coming forth. And the spectators—especially those of the lower classes, who were mostly Saxons—were heard to murmur among themselves; for the victorious challengers were the hated Normans.

"The day is against England, my lord," said Cedric, a Saxon knight, in a tone of bitter disappointment to Athelstane his kinsman.

And all this while the voices of the heralds were shouting, "Stand forth, gallant knights! Fair eyes look upon your deeds!"

But no gallant knights stood forth. The peasants grumbled. And old knights and nobles whispered to each other sadly that in their young days the knights were more high-spirited.

Then a single trumpet suddenly sounded at the far end of the lists. All voices were hushed; and all eyes turned eagerly to see this new champion, who, as soon as the barriers were opened, paced quickly into the lists.

II.—THE NEW CHAMPION

This new knight was not much taller than the middle height, and seemed to be rather slender than very strongly made; but he rode a goodly steed that might have mounted a king. His suit of armour, too, was richly inlaid with gold, and the motto on his shield was the strange word, "Disinherited."

He saluted the prince and the ladies by gracefully lowering his lance; and there was something so youthful about him, that the multitude took him to their hearts at once.

"Touch Ralph de Vipont's shield!" the onlookers shouted to him. "He has the least sure seat!"

The champion, amid these well-meaning hints, moved on, ascended the platform, and, to the astonishment of all, rode straight up to the middle pavilion, and struck the shield of Brian de Bois-Guilbert *with the sharp end of his spear,* until it rang again.

Everybody was speechless at the young knight's daring, and none more astonished than the proud Templar himself, whom the new champion had challenged to this deathly fight.

In his heart Brian de Bois-Guilbert thought this new champion an impertinent young spark; but for all that he took care to choose a fresh horse—a horse, too, of great strength and spirit. And he also chose a new and tough spear.

Soon the two champions stood opposite each other at the two ends of the lists, and the sightseers grew eager and anxious. That the Disinherited Knight would fall, nobody doubted for a moment; but they loved him for his courage and his gallantry.

The trumpets now sounded the signal for the combat to begin, and like lightning the champions vanished from their posts, and met in the centre of the lists with the shock as of a thunderbolt. The lances burst into shivers, and it seemed at the moment that both knights had fallen, for the shock had made each horse recoil upon its haunches.

But their clever riders soon pulled, them to their feet again, while the multitude shouted "Hurrah!" and the nobles cried, "Bravely done!" and the ladies waved their scarves and handkerchiefs.

The two champions having glared at each other with eyes that seemed to flash fire, each retired to the ends of the lists, and received a fresh lance from the attendants. Again the trumpets sounded the signal, and again the champions leaped from their stations and closed in the centre of the lists.

The Templar aimed at the middle of the young knight's shield, and struck it so fair that his spear went to shivers, and the stranger reeled in his saddle. On the other hand, the Disinherited Knight had directed the point of his lance towards the Templar's shield; but, changing his aim like lightning, he struck at the helmet instead.

Fair and true he hit the Norman on the visor—the part of the helmet which covered the face, with holes or bars for the wearer to see through—and Brian de Bois-Guilbert, in struggling to keep his seat, burst the girths of his saddle; and horse and man rolled on the ground. The multitude screamed and clapped.

It was the work of a moment for the Templar to disentangle himself from the stirrups and his fallen steed; and stung with madness, first at his disgrace, and then at the delight with which the people hailed it, he drew his sword, and waved it in defiance.

The Disinherited Knight immediately sprang from his horse, and he, too, unsheathed his sword.

The marshals of the field, however, spurred their horses between them, crying, "The laws of this tournament do not permit an encounter with swords!"

So the Disinherited Knight went back to his own end of the lists, and without getting off his horse he called for a bowl of wine; and, opening only the lower part of his helmet so that his face could not be seen, he cried, "To all true English hearts, and to the confusion of foreign tyrants!" and drank it off.

Meanwhile, in an agony of despair, the proud Templar hid himself in his own tent.

The Disinherited Knight then commanded his trumpet to be blown again, and told a herald to cry that he would willingly fight the other challengers if they came to him in turn.

At that, the tall and strong Front-de-Bœuf first took the field. And once again the huge multitude seemed hardly to breathe, while Cedric the Saxon, with his body half stretched over the balcony, awaited the encounter with his very heart and soul.

Horse and man rolled on the ground.

Even the lazy Athelstane called for a goblet of wine, and, quaffing it, shouted, "To the health of the Disinherited Knight!"

Both the champions broke their lances fairly; but as Front-de-Bœuf lost a stirrup, the marshals declared the Disinherited Knight to be the victor.

With the next three challengers the stranger was equally successful, always gaining some slight advantage. Indeed, in the last fight Ralph de Vipont was hurled to the ground.

Thousands of throats took up one after the other the cry, "The Disinherited Knight! The Disinherited Knight!" And, "His is the prize!" And Cedric, his whole face beaming with delight, shouted to Athelstane, "The day is *for* England, my lord!"

EXERCISES

1. Describe the picture on page 119. How could you tell from the picture that it is not a present-day scene?
2. Why was the Disinherited Knight a favourite with the populace watching the tournament?
3. Draw a plan of the tournament ground from the information given in the extracts.
4. What difference did it make if the challenger's shield were touched with the sharp or the reverse end of the lance?
5. Why did Cedric change his remark from "The day is against England" to "The day is *for* England"?

   Fill in the blanks:
   (a) The story deals with the period —— hundred years before the —— of Columbus to the New World.
   (b) The majority of the —— were Normans, whereas most of the multitude were ——.
   (c) The result of the —— was a great surprise to —— himself, as well as to most of the ——.
   (d) Although the —— wore armour, he could see through the —— of his helmet.
   (e) At the time of the ——, Richard Lion ——, having left the —— Land, where he had been fighting in the Crusades against the ——, was on his way back to ——.

LESSON 20

THE DWELLING

IN our hygiene lessons we have so far considered cleanliness, exercise and rest, the blood, disease, germs and parasites, hook-worm, malaria, the house-fly, air, water, and food. We will now pass to the subject of the dwelling—the place, whether palace or hut, in which people live. In doing so we will see what rules should be applied to all dwellings, and how these should be constructed in order to make them healthy places to live in.

Fortunately in the tropics we experience no extreme cold, which makes the warming and the ventilation of buildings a difficult matter in cold climates. In our houses practically all we have to consider is:

(1) how to secure plenty of fresh air and sunlight;

(2) how to keep out rain and mosquitoes; and

(3) not allowing more people to live in the house than it can contain safely, having regard to the health of its inhabitants.

A sufficient number of windows or jalousies must be provided to admit fresh air and sunlight. The doors, which are usually left open, except at night, also give entrance to these necessary aids to health. You have already learned why fresh air and sunlight are necessary—to kill disease germs, to keep away noxious insects, and to make the blood rich in oxygen and so keep us healthy and able to fight against any disease which may attack us.

Overcrowding in dwellings is extremely bad. Too many people living, and especially sleeping, in one room, brings about ill-health. It assists diseases in their attacks, and makes the occupants weak and feeble, because they are continually breathing bad air containing poisonous gases and other materials that their bodies have given off. Each person must have his requisite amount of air and space. It is not necessary for the rooms to be large, provided the air can pass in and out freely. Small rooms are quite healthy if the air they contain is being constantly changed without making draughts to cause chill, and if they are not overcrowded. There is, however, much over-crowding in the "barrack-yards" of some of our tropical towns, and much evil results from it.

Ventilation, therefore, is just as important in tropical dwellings as in those of colder climates, but it is much simpler to attain, as our climate allows us to let in the air freely at all times, provided that our bodies are sufficiently protected by proper clothing at night, and that we keep out mosquitoes, and prevent the rain entering during the wet season.

The site on which a dwelling is to be erected needs careful selection. In order that it may not be damp, it should be chosen where the ground-water (the water that has soaked into the ground after rains) can drain away quickly.

Between the small grains of soil near the surface, there is a quantity of air known as "ground-air." As the ground-water rises, this air is forced up and out of the soil. Having been contaminated with various substances in the earth, it is bad air and dangerous to breathe, and so should be kept out of the dwelling. Therefore, if it can possibly be avoided, the floor of the house should not be on the ground; but if the floor cannot be raised, then it should be made of something such as concrete or very hard-beaten mud, which will not let the ground-air pass through it.

A house made of wood, and with a galvanized iron roof, should be built on pillars of concrete, at least three or four feet high, so that the wind can pass freely under it to drive away the damp ground-air. The dwelling should, if possible, face the direction of the prevailing wind, east or north-east generally, so as to ensure a good current of fresh air right through the house. A wide gallery or verandah all round helps to keep off the sun and rain, and enables the doors and windows to be left open. It also provides accommodation for the people to sit out in the cool fresh air as much as possible.

In districts where mosquitoes are prevalent the windows and doors should have wire-gauze screens, or, better still, the verandah itself should be completely proofed in this way against mosquitoes. The ceiling of each room should contain a wire-gauze ventilator to allow the hot, impure air, which rises to the top of the room, to escape.

The out-offices and kitchen should be built to one side of the back of the house, so that the wind may not blow from them into the dwelling. All refuse should be put into a box or other covered receptacle, which should be emptied frequently, and the rubbish properly disposed of.

As many of these points as possible should also be considered in building a native peasant house or hut of the common style. These dwellings are often on the ground, but in such cases the floor should be raised at least one foot above the surface of the surrounding soil, and be composed of earth beaten so hard as not to allow the ground-air and ground-water to penetrate. It should have an even surface with a gentle slope towards the door, for it is easy to keep such a floor dry, and all dirt and insects can be easily swept out.

The walls of a mud house should be made as strong as possible, and their inner surface should be smooth. It is also important to make a curved junction between the wall and the floor, so that dust and insects may not collect in the corners. When small cracks appear in the floor or the walls they should be re-covered with mud. Insects like to hide in such places, and some, such as ticks, crawl out at night and bite those who are sleeping in the house. The floor should be sprinkled with water and brushed out every day to prevent jiggers and ticks from living there.

The rooms should, if possible, face the breeze, and there must be sufficient windows and doors to admit enough sunlight and fresh air for all the occupants to have a proper amount. Many village houses are much too dark and are not well ventilated.

Whenever possible the roof should be made of galvanized iron or shingles, as such a roof can be kept clean, and it serves to collect good water for storing in tanks. In many places, however, thatched roofs of carat or timite leaves, cane-trash or tapia grass, are the only kinds available. The thatch should be put on evenly and tightly to allow the rain to run off easily, and the edge of the roof should be brought down low enough to protect the walls. The rooms should be separated from the roof by flat ceilings made of boards, or laths of split branches of trees daubed with clay or mud, known as "wattle and daub."

In country places, where the sanitary cart does not remove the refuse, a site should be selected some distance away on the leeward side of the house or village, where the rubbish can be dumped and burned from time to time. When this is not possible the refuse should be dug into the ground.

The closets or latrines should be placed away from the houses, also to leeward, and far from any well or other water supply. They should be very carefully built, made fly-proof, and emptied as required. It is a good plan to place kerosene oil in them at intervals to kill the larvae of mosquitoes and flies which may be developing there.

EXERCISES

1. What are the points to consider in selecting the site for a dwelling?
2. What do you mean by *ventilation*? Explain why it is necessary.
3. Draw a plan of a house, indicating the different rooms and the kitchen and outhouses, and mark by an arrow the direction of the prevailing wind.
4. Give as many reasons as you can why an iron or shingle roof is better than a thatched one.
5. How should refuse be dealt with
    (*a*) in towns?
    (*b*) in the country or small villages?
6. Explain why the floor of the dwelling should be raised above the level of the ground.

LESSON 21

PICTURE LESSONS—IV

The Wood-Sawyers

How different this picture is in style from that of "Joan of Arc"! Here there are no small parts most carefully drawn, but only strong and vigorous masses of colour.

Millet, the painter of "The Wood-Sawyers" was the son of a French peasant. He was always poor, though now his pictures are worth enormous sums; he lived the life of a peasant among the country labourers whom he so often painted, and whose hard life he knew so well. You studied another of his pictures, "The Sheepfold" in Book IV.

Let us see how Millet composed this picture, "The Wood-Sawyers" to bring out the action and the sense of hard work, and at the same time to join the parts together by means of lines and colours. First, as you may see by the sketch on page 128, a line can be drawn from one sawyer to the other, passing through the woodman in the background, while the two ends of the trunk are so turned as to carry curves in the same direction. Other lines from the edges of the cut wood swing together to join these lines and to add force and grace to them.

As we have seen in other pictures, such as "The Fighting *Téméraire*" there is frequently one point to which many lines are drawn, and in "The Wood-Sawyers" this lies near the left-hand upper corner. You see at once that if lines are made to run together in this graceful manner, the figures

THE WOOD-SAWYERS. (*J. F. Millet.*)

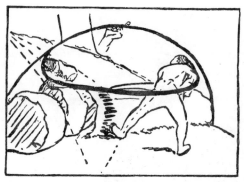

are more likely to compose or come together happily than if the artist were to paint without such careful thought.

Then an artist considers light and shade. There are no rules to guide him, but he finds by experience that a certain amount of light looks well against a certain degree of dark colour. Look how splendidly the white shirt of the sawyer stands out against the dark background, and how the light falling on the tree trunk contrasts with the shade on the ground. And the artist thought just as earnestly about the colours he used, so as to have a happy and harmonious composition.

Just one more point. The saw has reached the end of one sweep just at the moment when the woodman in the background is about to strike the tree. The artist has caught the moment of rest. We feel that immediately the blow will fall and the saw move—a very fine point in this composition.

EXERCISE

The picture suggests the story of the woodman's day. Try to tell it as simply as possible.

LESSON 22

DESCRIPTIVE EXTRACTS—I

PORT OF SPAIN IN 1869

Introduction.—This description is adapted from the pages of Kingsley's *At Last*—the title meaning that at last Kingsley was to see the West Indies and the Spanish Main, whose scenes had fired his imagination from childhood. Here, from the pen of that master of description, we shall find pictures of the people and the city of Port of Spain, Trinidad's capital, as they were in the middle of the nineteenth century. In reading the lesson you should compare and contrast the conditions in 1869 with those of the West Indies of the present day.

THE first thing notable, on landing in Port of Spain at the low quay which has just been reclaimed from the mud of the gulf, is the multitude of people who are doing nothing. It is not that they have taken an hour's holiday to see the packet come in. You will find them, or their duplicates, in the same places to-morrow and the next day. They stand idle in the market-place, not because they have not been hired, but because they do not want to be hired; being able to live, like the lazzaroni of Naples, on "midshipman's half-pay—nothing a day, and find yourself."

Next, the stranger will remark, here as at Grenada, that every one he passes looks strong, healthy, and well-fed. One meets few or none of those figures and faces, small, skinny, and haggard, which disgrace the so-called civilization of a British city. Nowhere in Port of Spain will you see such human beings as in certain streets of London, Liverpool, or Glasgow. Every one can live and thrive if they choose; and very pleasant it is to know that.

The road leads on past the custom-house, and you cross the pretty "Marine Square," with its fountain and flowering trees, and beyond them on the right the Roman Catholic cathedral, a stately building, with palmistes standing as tall sentries round; soon you go up a straight street, with a glimpse of a large English church, which must have been more handsome than now before its tall steeple was shaken down by an earthquake.

Next comes a glimpse, too, of large—even too large—Government buildings, brick-built, pretentious, without beauty of form. But however ugly in itself a building may be in Trinidad, it is certain, at least after a few years, to look beautiful, when embowered among noble flowering trees, like those that fill "Brunswick Square" and surround the great church on its south side.

Under cool porticoes and through tall doorways are seen dark stores, filled with all manner of good things from Britain or from the United States. These older-fashioned houses, built, I presume, on the Spanish model, are not without a certain stateliness. Their doors and windows reach almost to the ceiling, and ought to be plain proofs, to the eyes of certain discoverers of the "giant cities of Bashan,"* that the old Spanish and French colonists were nine or ten feet high apiece.

On the doorsteps sit negresses in gaudy print dresses, with stiff turbans (which are, according to this year's fashion, of chocolate and yellow silk plaid painted with

---

* An ancient district of Palestine, the location of whose cities is largely a matter of conjecture. Its giant king, Og, figures in Jewish tradition. (See *Deuteronomy*.)

thick yellow paint, and cost in all some four dollars), all aiding in the general work of doing nothing; save where here and there one sells, or tries to sell, sweetmeats, strange fruits, and junks of sugar-cane, to be gnawed by the dawdlers in mid-street, while they carry on their heads everything and anything, from half a barrow-load of yams to a saucer or a beer-bottle.

When you have ceased looking at the women and their ways, you become aware of the strange variety of races which people the city. Here passes a Coolie Hindu, with nothing on but his *dhoti* round his loins, and a scarf over his head; a white-bearded, delicate-featured old gentleman, his thin limbs and small hands and feet contrasting strangely with the brawny negroes round. There comes a bright-eyed young lady, probably his daughter-in-law, hung all over with bangles, in a white muslin petticoat, crimson cotton-velvet jacket, and green gauze veil, with her naked brown baby astride on her hip; a clever, smiling, delicate little woman, who is quite aware of the brightness of her own eyes.

And who are these three boys in dark blue coatees and trousers, one of whom carries, hanging at one end of a long bamboo, a couple of sweet potatoes, at the other possibly a pebble to balance them? As they approach, their doleful visage betrays them. Chinese they are, without a doubt.

There, again, is a group of coloured men of all ranks, talking eagerly, business, or even politics; some of them as well dressed as if they were fresh from Europe; some of them, too, six feet high, and broad in proportion; as fine a race, physically, as one would wish to look upon; and with no want of shrewdness either, or determination, in their faces: a race who ought, if they will be wise and virtuous, to have before them a great future.

Here come home from the convent school two young ladies; and here comes the unmistakable Englishman, tall, fair, close-shaven, arm-in-arm with another man, whose more delicate features, more sallow complexion, and little moustache, mark him as some Frenchman or Spaniard of old family.

The straight and level street, swarming with dogs, vultures, chickens, and goats, passes now out of the old into the newer part of the city, and the type of the houses changes at once. Some are mere wooden sheds of one or two rooms, comfortable enough in such a climate, where a sleeping-place is all that is needed—if the occupiers would but keep them clean. Other houses, wooden too, belong to well-to-do folk. Over high walls you catch sight of jalousies and verandahs, inside which must be most delightful darkness and coolness.

But what would—or at least ought to—strike the new-comer's eye with most pleasurable surprise, and make him realize into what a new world he has been suddenly translated, are the flowers which show over the walls on each side of the street. In that little garden, not thirty feet broad, what treasures there are! A tall palm—whether palmiste or oil-palm—has its smooth trunk hung all over with orchids, tied on with wire. Close to it stands a purple Dracæna, such as are put on English dinner-tables in pots— but this one is twenty feet high; and next to it is that strange tree, the Clavija, of which the Creoles are justly fond.

A single straight stem, fifteen feet high, carries huge oblong leaves atop, and beneath them, growing out of the stem itself, delicate panicles of little white flowers, fragrant exceedingly. A double blue pea and a purple Bignonia are scrambling over shrubs and walls. And what is this which hangs over into the road, some fifteen feet in height— long, bare, curving sticks, carrying each at its end a flat blaze of scarlet? What but the Poinsettia, paltry scions of which, like the Dracæna, adorn our hothouses and dinner-tables. The street is on fire with it all the way up, now in mid-winter; while at the street end opens out a green park, fringed with noble trees in full leaf; underneath them more pleasant little suburban villas; and behind all, again, a background of steep, wooded mountain a thousand feet in height. That is the Savannah, the public park and race-ground; such as neither London nor Paris can boast.

La Brea

Introduction.—The following description of the Trinidad Pitch Lake is also taken from Kingsley's *At Last*. Although written in 1869, it still presents a very true picture of the lake itself, for it is only the works, residences, and transport appliances which Kingsley would find so much changed were he to revisit the spot. Before reading it, you should revise Lesson 35 in Book IV.

At last we surmounted the last rise, and before us lay the famous lake—not at the bottom of a depression, as we expected, but at the top of a rise, where the ground slopes away from it on two sides, and rises from it very slightly on the two others. The black pool glared and glittered in the sun. A group of islands, some twenty yards wide, were scattered about the middle of it. Beyond it rose a noble forest of Moriche fan palms; and to the right of them high wood with giant Mombins and undergrowth of Cocorite—a paradise on the other side of the Stygian pool.

We walked, with some misgivings, on the asphalt, and found it perfectly hard. In a few yards we were stopped by a channel of clear water, with tiny fish and water beetles in it, and looking round, saw that the whole lake was intersected with channels, so unlike anything that can be seen elsewhere, that it is not easy to describe them.

Conceive a crowd of mushrooms, of all shapes, from ten to fifty feet across, close together side by side, their tops being kept at exactly the same level, their rounded rims squeezed tight against each other; then conceive water poured on them so as to fill the parting seams, and in the wet season, during which we visited it, to overflow the tops somewhat. Thus would each mushroom represent, tolerably well, one of the innumerable flat asphalt bosses, which seem to have sprung up each from a separate centre, while the parting seams would be of much the same shape as those in the asphalt, broad and shallow atop, and rolling downward in a smooth curve, till they are at bottom mere cracks, from two to ten feet deep.

We pushed on across the lake, over the planks which the negroes laid down from island to island.

Passing these little islands, which are said (I know not how truly) to change their places and numbers, we came to the very fountain of Styx, to that part of the lake where the asphalt is still oozing up.

As the wind set towards us, we soon became aware of an evil smell—petroleum and sulphuretted hydrogen at

THE PITCH LAKE, LA BREA—GENERAL VIEW.

once—which gave some of us a headache. The pitch here is yellow and white with sulphur foam; so are the water channels; and out of both water and pitch innumerable bubbles of gas arise, loathsome to the smell. We became aware also that the pitch was soft under our feet. We left the impression of our boots; and if we had stood awhile, we should soon have been ankle deep. No doubt there are spots where, if a man stayed long enough, he would be slowly and horribly engulfed.

CHARLES KINGSLEY.

EXERCISES

1. Give a description, such as a stranger might write, of the chief city of your country, with Kingsley's description of Port of Spain as a model.
2. What differences would Kingsley notice in the main streets of any of our West Indian cities were he to revisit it to-day?
3. Describe any garden you know. Try to imitate Kingsley's description of the garden.
4. Were the old French and Spanish colonists really nine or ten feet tall? What did Kingsley mean by this?
5. Make a list of all the trees and plants named in this lesson. Which of them do you know?
6. Compare Kingsley's description with the picture of the Pitch Lake. What differences do you notice? In what ways are they similar?
7. Make sentences of your own containing the following words:

haggard	unmistakable	impression
stateliness	realize	oozing
astride	paradise	moustache
visage	innumerable	civilization

8. The word "people" is usually a noun. In this lesson it is also used as another part of speech. What is it? Why?
9. Make a list of the ten words in this lesson which cause you the most difficulty to spell (names of plants not included).

LESSON 23

"HAMLET, PRINCE OF DENMARK"

Introduction.—Shakespeare did not write for young boys and girls, but for grown men and women. For this reason you cannot yet fully understand and appreciate his works. Nevertheless I think you would like to read two of the stories which are told in his plays. I shall first tell you the story of Shakespeare's greatest tragedy, *Hamlet, Prince of Denmark*, then that of his beautiful comedy, *As You Like It*. You already know that a tragedy is a grave and sad play.

I

ONCE upon a time there was a good King of Denmark who died suddenly, leaving his son Hamlet as heir to the throne. Less than two months after the king's death his widowed queen took another husband. She married the late king's brother Claudius, who was the very opposite in every respect of her former husband. He had been brave and noble, handsome and upright; while Claudius was mean in character and mind, and had no graces of person or manner.

The young prince had loved and almost worshipped his father, and was heartbroken at his loss. The marriage of his mother made him even more sad. Between grief for his father's memory and shame at his mother's marriage, he fell into a deep sadness and gloom, from which nothing could rouse him.

His mother and his uncle tried in every way to divert his mind, but he refused to be comforted. He still dressed himself in the deepest mourning, and would not change it even on the day of the queen's marriage.

He took no part in the wedding feast, and gave his mother no words of good will. To him her marriage day appeared to be a day of shame and disgrace.

What troubled him most was the manner of his father's death. Claudius said that a serpent had stung the king to death, but Hamlet could not help thinking that the serpent who had stung him now sat on his throne.

One day a friend of the young prince told him that a figure exactly like the dead king, his father, had been seen two or three times at midnight by the sentinels who watched on the battlements of the castle. The figure, so the soldiers said, was clad from head to foot in the dead king's armour; its face was sad and pale, and its brown beard was turning grey. When they spoke to it they received no reply, though once it appeared as if about to speak. At the moment when the cock crowed the figure vanished out of their sight.

This story greatly disturbed the mind of the young prince, and he could not but believe that it was his father's ghost. He felt sure that it had come to speak to him, so he determined to watch with the sentinels the very next night.

When darkness fell, he took his stand with his friend Horatio on the battlements and waited. The night was chilly, and the air was very raw. Just as Hamlet was talking about the coldness of the night the ghost appeared.

In a moment Hamlet knew that it was his father. At first he was overcome with fear, but he soon recovered himself, and crying out, "King! father!" begged the ghost to say why it had left the grave, and to tell him what he was to do in order to give peace to the disturbed spirit. Then the ghost beckoned Hamlet to follow him.

JOHN KEMBLE, A GREAT ENGLISH ACTOR, AS "HAMLET."
(*From the painting by Sir Thomas Lawrence, P.R.A.*)

When they were alone and unobserved the spirit spoke, and said that it was indeed the ghost of the dead king, who had been cruelly murdered by his brother Claudius. As he was sleeping in the garden one afternoon, his wicked brother had crept up to him, poured poison into his ear, and thus robbed him of life.

Then the ghost called upon Hamlet to revenge this foul murder, and this the trembling prince promised to do. After beseeching him not to harm his mother in any way, the vision vanished, and Hamlet found himself alone.

II

Hamlet now made a solemn vow that thenceforth he would devote himself wholly to the work of avenging his dead father. He had been weak and miserable before the appearance of the ghost; now he felt that his mind was giving way.

He feared that if he lost his reason he would be unable to do the ghost's bidding, so he resolved to *pretend* to be mad. In this way he hoped that his uncle would not suspect that he knew the dreadful secret, and would think him incapable of plotting revenge.

From this time onward Hamlet behaved as though he were really out of his wits. He spoke and dressed in the strangest manner, and so well did he act that the king and queen were both deceived. At first they thought that grief at his father's death had driven him mad, but after a while they came to the conclusion that he had lost his reason because he was unhappy in love.

Before Hamlet's grief had so changed him he dearly loved a fair maid named Ophelia, the daughter of Polonius, the king's chief counsellor. Hamlet had begged the lady to marry him, and she believed that he really loved her.

When, however, he became oppressed by grief he began to treat Ophelia with unkindness, and almost with rudeness. As a matter of fact, Hamlet still loved Ophelia, but he tried to set his love aside because he thought that it would interfere with his vow of revenge.

He could not, however, put Ophelia entirely out of his thoughts, and one day he wrote her a letter that really seemed to be the work of a madman. Here and there, however, there were gentle words which showed that his love for her was not dead.

Ophelia showed this letter to her father, and the old man took it to the king and queen. When they read it they felt sure that poor Ophelia was the cause of Hamlet's madness, and they hoped that her love would soon restore him to health of mind and body.

You and I know that it was not Hamlet's love for Ophelia which had so changed him. Every hour of the day he thought of his poor dead father and of his solemn promise to avenge the murder. But Hamlet was a man of weak resolution, and he could not make up his mind how or when to bring Claudius to justice. He hated the thought of killing him, yet he had sworn to do it.

Then, too, he began to wonder whether, after all, he had really seen and spoken to his father's ghost, or had only been visited by a bad dream. So he wavered day by day, and at last decided that he would not kill the king until he had other and better grounds for believing him guilty.

While Hamlet was in this distracted frame of mind a company of actors arrived at the castle. They were well known to the young prince, who in the days of his happiness had greatly delighted in their plays.

He now welcomed them warmly, and begged one of the players, who was an old friend, to recite a favourite speech. The actor began his recitation, and so completely did he throw himself into the spirit of it that real tears began to fall from his eyes.

This set Hamlet thinking about the powerful effect of the actor's art on those who see and hear him. Suddenly he remembered a story of a man who had killed a companion, and who went to the theatre, where he saw a play in which a murder was performed. When the murderer saw the actor being put to death in the same way that he had killed his victim, he sprang from his seat and confessed his crime.

At once Hamlet thought that he might set a trap for the king in this manner, and learn from his behaviour whether the ghost's story was true or false. He immediately arranged with the actors to perform a play showing the murder of the late king, and invited Claudius and his mother to be present. While the play was going on he meant to watch his uncle very closely.

The play took place that very evening. As the story unfolded itself, both the king and the queen were very uncomfortable. At the moment when one of the players

THE PLAY SCENE IN "HAMLET."
(From the painting by D. Maclise, R.A.)

was pouring poison into the ear of his sleeping brother, the king sprang from his seat, and crying out that he was unwell, retired to his private chamber.

The play thus came to a sudden end; and Hamlet became strangely excited, for he was now quite certain that the ghost's words were true, and that Claudius was his father's murderer.

III

The king was very uneasy, for he suspected that Hamlet had somehow discovered his secret. He therefore bade the queen send for her son and question him closely. In order that he might learn how much Hamlet knew, he instructed Polonius to hide behind the curtains and to report to him all that passed between the queen and the young prince. Polonius was a crafty old man, and was quite willing to play the spy.

The queen told her son that he had given great offence to his *father*. At once Hamlet interrupted her, and said that he would not give that honoured name to his uncle. "Mother," he said, "*you* have much offended *my father*." At this the queen grew angry, and was about to retire, when Hamlet seized her by the wrist and detained her.

Old Polonius, behind the curtains, feared that Hamlet was about to show violence to his mother, so he cried out for help. Then Hamlet knew that he was being spied upon; and, whipping out his sword, thrust it through and

OPHELIA.
(From the painting by Sir John E. Millais, P.R.A.)

through the curtain, shouting madly, "How now! a rat? Dead! for a ducat,* dead!"

Polonius was indeed dead, and Hamlet, though sorry for his rash deed, pretended not to care. He pleaded with the queen in most moving words, and told her how wicked she had been to forget his father and to marry the man who had murdered him. Then he showed her two pictures—the one of the late king, the other of the present king—and bade her mark the difference.

What a grace was on the brow of his father! how like a god he was! This man, he said, *had* been her husband. Then he showed her the man who had usurped his father's place. How like a blight or a mildew he looked! How unworthy he was in every way to be her husband! At this the queen begged him to cease, and said that his words pierced her heart like daggers.

At this moment the ghost of the late king again appeared. Hamlet saw the vision clearly, but it was invisible to his mother. The ghost then spoke to Hamlet, and said that he had come to remind him of his promise and to whet his almost blunted purpose. Then he bade Hamlet speak to his mother, who was fainting with fright.

Hamlet thereupon begged his mother for the future to avoid Claudius, and said that when she should show herself mindful of his father's memory he would ask a blessing of her as a son. The queen promised to do so, and Hamlet departed.

The murder of Polonius soon came to the ears of the king, who would have put Hamlet to death if his mother

---

* An old gold coin worth about two dollars of our money.

had not pleaded for him. In the end the young prince was banished to England; but on the voyage he was captured by pirates, who showed him much kindness, and set him ashore again on Danish ground. Hamlet at once wrote to the king, saying that he was about to return home.

Next day Hamlet and his friend Horatio passed a churchyard, in which they saw a man digging a grave. Hamlet talked with the gravedigger, and as he did so a funeral procession appeared. Then he learnt to his great grief that Ophelia was dead and was about to be buried.

Her father's violent end and the- unkindness of Hamlet had robbed her of her reason, and she had wandered from the court into the woods, where she had fallen into a stream and had been drowned. At the sight of her dead body all Hamlet's love for the poor lady returned.

Now Ophelia had an only brother, a proud and headstrong young man named Laertes. He had loved his sister very dearly, and he was almost frantic with grief at her death. When her body was lowered into the grave he sprang into it in order to hold his beloved sister once more in his arms. Then Hamlet sprang into the grave too, and Laertes, knowing him to be the murderer of his father and the cause of his sister's death, grappled fiercely with him.

The attendants parted them with difficulty, and the poor heart-broken prince cried:

> "I loved Ophelia: forty thousand brothers
> Could not, with all their quantity of love.
> Make up the sum."

The wicked uncle now determined that Hamlet should die, so he secretly sent for Laertes and plotted with him. He persuaded the young man to challenge Hamlet to a friendly bout of fencing; and as Hamlet was proud of his skill, he gladly agreed to the match. A day was appointed for the sword-play, and when it arrived the king and queen and all the courtiers were present.

The foils with which the young men were to fence had buttons at the end to make them harmless. The king instructed Laertes to break off the button of his foil, and to rub poison on the blade, so that, even if Hamlet were scratched, he would die.

The fight began, and Laertes, who was the better swordsman, played with Hamlet and let him gain some advantages. Then after a few passes he made a deadly thrust at the young prince, and pierced him with the poisoned blade. A scuffle followed, during which both the swords were struck out of the fencers' hands, and when they snatched them up again Hamlet seized the foil which Laertes had used. Then the fighting was resumed, and Hamlet managed to wound Laertes with his own weapon.

At this moment the queen shrieked out that she was poisoned. The wicked king had prepared a bowl of poisoned wine for Hamlet to drink when he was hot and thirsty with the sword-play. The queen had tasted the wine, and was now in the throes of death.

Hamlet knew that there was treachery on foot, and he ordered the doors to be shut while he sought for the traitor. Then Laertes, repenting of his part in the wickedness, told Hamlet that he too was poisoned, and that it was the king who was the traitor. At once Hamlet turned upon his false uncle, and stabbed him to the heart.

And so, with all the chief actors in the tragedy dead or dying, the mournful play concludes. Horatio would willingly have died with his friend, but Hamlet bade him live to tell his story to the world. Then the young prince died, and Horatio wept bitter tears and commended his soul to God. Thus ends the miserable story.

EXERCISES

1. Why is this play called a tragedy? What is the opposite of a tragedy?
2. Write out a list of the chief persons in *Hamlet,* and in a few words, such as you would find on a playbill, describe each character. Begin thus:

   THE KING .... The ruler of Denmark.
   HAMLET.................... His son, the heir to the throne.
   THE QUEEN............... etc.

3. Say how each of the following came by their death: Polonius, Laertes, the Queen, Claudius, and Hamlet.
4. The Latin verb *fero* means "I bear." There are many English words which contain this Latin word in the form of *fer*—as re*fer* or of*fer.* Write down six other words containing *fer.*
5. Describe the coloured picture on page 145. Your picture lessons in this book will help you to appreciate this masterpiece. Which part is the "centre of interest" in the picture? How has the artist drawn attention to it?
6. Make one sentence out of each of the following pairs, by using sentence-joiners:

   Polonius was a crafty old man; he was quite willing to play the spy.
   At this the queen grew angry; she was about to leave the room.

Polonius was indeed dead; Hamlet pretended not to care.

The fight began; Laertes played with Hamlet.

Divide the sentences you have made into subject, predicate, and object (if any).

7. Make a list of the twelve most difficult words in this lesson. (Names of persons not included.) Learn to spell them, and then use each one in a sentence of your own.

LESSON 24

THE LIVING PLANT—III

FRUITS

IN the lesson dealing with flowers we saw that if the tiny structures called ovules within the ovaries were fertilized by the grains of pollen, growth would take place and fruits and seeds be produced. We saw, too, in Book IV., when reading of the "Dispersal of Seeds," that the fruit plays an important part in distributing its seeds.

The term "fruit" in its true sense means that part of the plant which contains the seeds, whether it is edible or not; in everyday life the term is often merely applied to such fruit as we can eat, although this is not its full meaning.

The fruit is really the mature or fully-grown ovary, which forms a case for the seeds. It develops from the pistil after fertilization, when the petals and other parts, having done their work, have withered and fallen.

Fruits usually consist of two distinct layers, an outer layer forming a tough skin, and an inner one, the edible portion which surrounds the seeds. You can see these two layers in the diagram showing the section of a papaw Often there are three layers, as in the case of the mango.

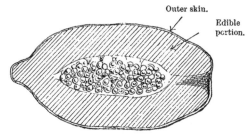

Section of Papaw Fruit.

The skin forms the outer layer, which acts as a protective covering, the edible pulp the middle layer, and the hard shell the inner layer. Inside the hard shell lies the seed, covered by a very thin seed-coat. Sometimes the different layers are not readily distinguishable.

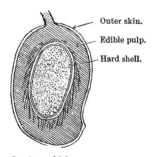

Section of Mango.

There are many different kinds of fruits; they may contain but one seed, as does the coconut, or may have many seeds, as has the papaw. The fruits of the sugar-apple and the custard-apple are really a cluster of one-seeded fruits tightly packed together. The pea family is readily recognized by its pods or legumes; among the numerous members of this family are the pigeon-pea, salad beans, and the pois doux.

In another lesson you learned that seeds are often provided with wings to aid their dispersal. In the same manner some fruits themselves are winged. The balsam of Peru, the porcupine tree, and the Easter flower are good examples of plants which have winged fruits.

Fruits vary in the manner in which they open and release their seeds. They split in various ways; sometimes they open in a lengthwise manner like beans; occasionally the top of the fruit comes off like a cap, as in the Portulaca, the plant often known as "jump-up-and-kiss-me"; others open in ways just as strange and interesting.

Easter Flower and Winged Fruit.

Some fruits rarely develop seeds. Bananas and plantains are well-known instances of this. If a banana is cut through the middle you can see little dark-coloured specks which are really the undeveloped seeds.

The navel orange does not bear seeds. This is unusual for oranges, and the discoverer of this characteristic, recognizing how valuable such a fruit would be when offered for sale, had the tree propagated by budding. It is now largely grown in many orange-growing countries, and the fruit is highly prized.

All plant structures which are commonly known as fruits are not really so; the moist, juicy part of the cashew is really the swollen fruit stalk, the fruit being the nut at the end of it. The pineapple is also a false fruit, in which

"Jump-up-and-kiss-me."

certain parts of the flower have become fleshy, the true fruit being the little pockets in which the seeds are found.

Many fruits are of great use to man. Large numbers of them are suitable for food and many have other uses. The coconut, besides having a useful nut, produces large quantities of fibre, which can be manufactured into such articles as rope and mats.

SEEDS

The seed is the beginning of the life of the young plant. It consists of a tiny plant with a reserve store of food-material to enable it to commence to grow until it can collect food for itself by means of its roots and leaves.

Cashew.

A seed is composed of several parts, the seed-coat, the seed-leaves, the young root, and the young shoot. To understand these fully, you should examine the seeds of both a bean and corn just after they commence to sprout.

Young Bean Plant.
(*a*, *b*, seed-leaves.)

The bean will have burst and thrown off its seed-coat, which serves as a protective covering. Two fleshy seed-leaves may be seen, which seem to be the two halves of the seed. In these were stored the food which enabled the seed to begin its growth. One main root has grown straight downwards, and has already begun to give off side branches. On these may be seen the tiny root hairs by which the plant collects its food.

In the bean the stem pushes up into the air in the form of an arch, which saves the young plant from damage in passing through the soil. As soon as the top of the stem is above the soil it straightens itself and begins to put forth leaves.

The maize or corn is different from the bean. In this case the seed-coat and the next layer of the fruit are so joined together as to be indistinguishable, and the seed-coat does not fall off when the seed germinates. The baby plant is produced at the pointed end of the seed, whilst the other and larger part is a store of plant food. This is made use of in a similar way to that in the seed-leaves of the bean.

You will notice, too, that the maize grain, unlike the bean seed, only produces one seed-leaf—all grasses being alike in this respect—and it pushes straight out of the soil.

Instead of one main root, a number of roots may be seen coming from the seed.

The plant food stored in the seeds of cereals, such as wheat, maize, and rice, is of great use to man, as it forms our principal food.

Although each seed contains a baby plant ready to grow, it will not do so unless supplied with air, warmth, and moisture. This you may test by giving them any two of these conditions without the other. Too much water in the soil would deprive the seeds of air for breathing, and they would rot instead of growing. Air without moisture would not allow the baby plant to make use of the plant food stored up in the seed. Warmth is necessary, but to a different degree with different plants. Most plants which grow in the tropics would die in a cold climate, and, similarly, plants which are accustomed to cold weather will not usually thrive in our countries. Each plant, therefore, requires the right amount of warmth, moisture, and air for its successful growth, not only as a seed, but all through its life.

Young Maize Plant.

·   ·   ·   ·   ·   ·

In our study of the "living plant" we have therefore seen that it is not only a thing of beauty, but is a real live organism, living its own life, growing, producing stems, leaves, flowers, fruits, and seeds, and thus making provision for the reproduction of similar plants later on. A great deal of life in the world, too, depends upon the wonderful work performed by plants in manufacturing their own food, for all animals, including ourselves, either live upon plants or feed upon other animals which do so.

EXERCISES

1. The longest word you have read so far is in this lesson. It contains seventeen letters, but it is not really difficult to spell. Divide it into its syllables.
2. What is the real meaning of the term "fruit"? Explain the difference between a seed and a fruit.
3. The banana has some seeds in the middle of the fruit, yet if they are planted they will not grow into new plants. Why?
4. Explain why the work which goes on in the leaves of plants is perhaps the most important work in the world.
5. What are the main differences between the seeds of the bean and corn? Why is the young stem of the bean in the form of an arch?
6. What does a seed consist of? Make a drawing of a seed which has just started to grow. Name the parts.
7. Four bottles, numbered 1, 2, 3, and 4, are arranged as follows:
   1. Two or three layers of wet blotting-paper are placed at the bottom, and some dry seeds of corn are put on them. The bottle is then corked and sealed.
   2. This bottle is prepared in the same way, but is left uncorked and open to the air.
   3. This bottle is prepared as No. 2, but afterwards placed in an ice-chest.
   4. The corn seeds and the inside of the bottle are first carefully dried. After the seeds are placed in the bottle it is then corked and sealed.

   In which of the bottles will the seed germinate and grow strongly? Explain why.

LESSON 25

A VISIT TO THE KAIETEUR FALL

Introduction.—The West Indies and the neighbouring countries on the mainland contain many wonderful works of Nature, but it is doubtful if any surpasses in grandeur the stupendous waterfall, known as the Kaieteur Fall, in the faraway interior of Guyana. Although it was discovered in 1870, very few people beyond the aboriginal Indians who inhabit the neighbourhood have seen this great natural wonder, owing to the difficulty and expense of the long journey from the coast-lands, where most of the people of the colony reside.

The fall is no less than five times as high as Niagara, which holds pride of place among the great waterfalls of the world, yet outside of Guyana comparatively few people know of its existence. It has a clear drop of 741 feet, after which it falls 88 feet more over a sloping rock, making a total height of 829 feet, while the width varies from 200 to 400 feet.

In the lesson on the gold and diamond fields, in Book IV., we journeyed to the neighbourhood by the Essequibo River, but on this occasion we shall take the alternative route up the Demerara River. You should compare the two routes on the map on page 12 of your West Indian Atlas.

"WE left Georgetown in the early morning by the Demerara river steamer, and through the day we journeyed up-stream, first past sugar estates with their tall chimneys and their vast stretches of vivid green sugar-cane, then past cacao and rubber estates with the managers' bungalows snuggling amid the trees, and then by alternate stretches of bush and savannah. All the way up were clearings here and there, where blacks and bovianders* had their little

---

* The boviander is a cross between the old Dutch inhabitant and the Indian.

houses on the river bank, and where they grew provisions to supply the daily food for the capital at the mouth. It was sunset when we arrived at Wismar, the steamer terminus, and here we found schooners loading the colony's greenheart logs to bear them over the world, and also a miniature railway-station with all its attendant bustle. Then we were borne across by the railway which leads to the Essequibo River, always along a reef of pure white sand and continually passing stations of wood-cutting grants. Rockstone was reached when darkness had fallen, and by oil-lamp we stored our baggage and were escorted to the little bungalow hotel, where a comfortable night was passed.

"Daybreak saw us out again, thanks to the shrill whistling of the Essequibo river launch, and once more we were on our way, pounding along hour by hour up the broad but shallow stream, steering from side to side to avoid sand-banks, now and again meeting batteaux* filled with gold workers or balata bleeders on their homeward route, and all the way passing an unbroken forest line which stretched down to the bank on either side in a canopy of impenetrable green.

"As evening fell, we turned into the tributary Potaro, and so we drove up-stream until the darkness deepened and we saw the lights of Tumatumari, the gold-town, twinkling ahead. A night spent there at the quarters of a hospitable gold official, a hasty view of the Tumatumari Falls at early morn, and once more we were off by another launch which lay waiting above the rapids.

---

* The local river boats are known as "batteaux."

"A few hours brought us to Potaro Landing, and here was an end of civilized travelling and the beginning of bush life. We took the trail through the forest, which avoided a large bend of the river, and brought us to a camping-place on the Pakatuk Rapids. A day might be spent in pulling and 'portaging' the long shallow wooden batteau which was now our means of conveyance over these, but the foreseeing organizer of a trip arranged that this should be done in advance, and so we found the batteau with its mixed black and Indian crew, paddles in hand, ready awaiting us.

"From this time onward the journey increased in interest daily. As we worked more and more south the forest-clad hills grew closer, and each reach of the river discovered fresh beauties of tropical life. The day's work was always much the same: the early start from camp before the rising sun had dispersed the river mist; the rhythmic and monotonous paddling mile by mile up-stream; the hauling of the boat over the rapids, when all stood waist deep in water and pulled, pushed, and lifted it over the barriers of rocks; the pitching of the camp in the evening among the trees on the river bank, when the pot was boiled and the pipe smoked; and finally the sleep in hammocks beneath the stars, when all was still save the night birds fluting in the branches overhead.

"Four days later we reached the Takuit Falls, and, as the river from here onward was unnavigable, we left the boat and started on our long, slow climb up the hill to the Kaieteur Tableland. The Indian path was steep and long and the forest air hot and heavy, so that we were glad at heart when we emerged on the rocky tableland. A short walk across brought us to the edge of the plateau basin, and then the Kaieteur Fall burst upon us in all its grandeur. From the highlands in the distance one could see the river rolling past forest and plain till it reached the edge of the tableland, and, hurling itself over, go thundering down into the mist below; then again, in the valley far beneath, one could see it meandering on its normal river course down through the lowlands to the sea.

"As for the fall itself, mere words can never adequately describe it. From the upper lip of the cliff the water glides over in a glassy curtain on its descent of near a thousand feet; and gradually the curtain splits and shivers in a hundred lines of falling water, which go shooting, feathering down and down until the eye can only see the mist which rises from the pool where the waters meet the lowlands in the dark depths far below. The wind-eddies blow the spray mist here and there and up and down, and the sun's rays catch the vapour cloud and throw across now one, now two, quivering rainbows; and flights of white-throated swallows continually sweep over the face of the fall, and shooting down with incredible velocity twist in and out of the gloomy cavern behind. Night and day there booms in one's ears the deep organ note of the fall, and around all is the solitude of nature, broken only by the passing of Indians on their hunting trips or travellers such as ourselves.

"The night we spent on the Kaieteur Plateau was a night one never could forget, when the moon rose up and with the cold white light touched the distant hills above, and the heavy forests down below, and clothed the fall in a ghostly garb that made one feel with the

KAIETEUR FALL.

Indians when in fear and reverence they pass from the presence of the Spirit of the Fall. And so it was with us; with a feeling of inexplicable humility and reverence we gazed our fill, and then next morning we packed our belongings and turned our backs upon one of the greatest and most beautiful works of Nature. Slowly we descended the hill again and paddled our way back day by day to the haunts of men, and so we returned to civilization with a new and happy memory indelibly engraven on our minds."

.   .   .   .   .   .

The name Kaieteur, or more properly Kaietuk, is an Indian word meaning the "Old Man" Fall. It is said to be due to the custom of the Indians of putting their relatives into a canoe when they got too feeble and old to work, and allowing them to drift down the river and over the fall. They also speak of the fall as "The God of Waters."

[This description, which is by Sir Edward Davson, has been extracted from *The British West Indies,* and is included by the courtesy of Sir Algernon Aspinall, Secretary, West India Committee.]

EXERCISES

1. Which words in the lesson have a similar meaning to:

covering	cleared
difficult to explain	always the same
unbelievable speed	came out
small	moving slowly along
whistling	permanently written

2. In this lesson you have *read* a description of the fall. It is now possible, however, to *see* a representation of this great cataract in motion. Where? Although you might see the fall

in action by this means, you would miss something which a visitor to the real fall would experience. What is that?

3. Draw a map of Guyana and show the route to the Kaieteur Fall.

4. Why is the journey to the fall a lengthy and difficult undertaking?

5. Study the picture on page 161, and then describe the fall in your own words.

6. To what is the name attributed? What reason can you give for the Indians referring to it as "The God of Waters"?

LESSON 26

PICTURE LESSONS — V

THE SURRENDER OF BREDA

THIS picture was painted in 1647 by a great Spanish artist, Velasquez. At that time the Spaniards were attacking the Netherlands, and they had taken and burnt many cities. The Spanish commander, Spinola, laid siege to the Flemish town of Breda, where the governor, Justin de Nassau, held out stubbornly for nearly a year, until at length he was obliged to give in.

The picture shows the moment when Justin comes to surrender the town. The two chief actors in the scene must be made as prominent as possible, so the artist places them in the middle of the picture, and proceeds to balance the crowd on either side.

Justin has come with only a few attendants, while Spinola has all his officers and a crowd of lancers with

THE SURRENDER OF BREDA. (*Velasquez.*)

him. The artist, therefore, brings the few Flemish soldiers nearer the front of the picture, where they appear larger, and thus, though few in number balance the more numerous Spaniards.

Both leaders have descended from their horses. Spinola is no braggart. He does not wish to add insult to defeat, and the artist has expressed this by surrounding and, as it were, hiding the two leaders from mere idle and curious onlookers. Each horseman has his page; but while the Flemish page looks down on the ground, the Spanish page lifts his head triumphantly.

See, too, how skilfully the artist suggests victory and defeat. The Flemish officers bear short staves, whilst the long Spanish lances are raised almost insolently. The very horses help in the story, for while one is stately and vigorous, the other looks mournfully out from the picture.

Velasquez has drawn attention in other ways to the two chief characters in his picture. You will notice that the Flemish officer in the foreground holds his staff slantingly. This helps to cut off most of the Flemish officers from Justin and his page. On the other side, you will see among the forest of spears that three of them are sloping in the opposite direction, so as to carry the eye down to Spinola; and the light flag on the right points directly to the centre of the composition.

———————

LESSON 27

"AS YOU LIKE IT"

Introduction.—In Lesson 23 you read the plot of *Hamlet*, and I am sure that you found it very sad and gloomy. Let us turn for relief to one of the bright and merry plays which Shakespeare wrote. In all he composed more than a dozen comedies, which still afford playgoers much amusement. These comedies are full of jokes, shrewd sayings, sweet songs, laughable muddles, and queer mistakes. One of the most delightful of them is called *As You Like It*. The story of this play you shall now hear.

I

ONCE upon a time a certain Duke ruled over one of the provinces in the north of France. The Duke had a younger brother named Frederick, who by all sorts of baseness and trickery managed to turn his people against him. As a result the Duke was driven from his dominions, and Frederick was chosen to rule in his stead. Gathering a few faithful friends about him, the banished Duke withdrew to the Forest of Arden, where he lived in the greenwood like the famous Robin Hood of old English story.

Now the banished Duke had an only daughter, named Rosalind; and the usurper had also an only daughter, named Celia. The two girls loved each other dearly, and could not bear to be separated even for an hour. So, when the Duke was driven away to the forest, Rosalind remained at her uncle's court as a companion to her cousin Celia.

One day the girls went to see a wrestling match which was to take place in a courtyard of the palace. The Duke's champion—a big, powerful man named Charles—was ready to meet all comers. He had overthrown many strong men in contests of this kind, and had maimed and even slain some of his opponents. Strange to say, a very young and unpractised man had challenged him, and now the struggle was about to begin.

The young ladies looked on with fear and trembling. As for Rosalind, her heart went out to the brave youth. Cheered by her kind words, he strove with all his might, and actually overthrew the champion, who was so much hurt that for a while he was unable to speak or move.

The Duke was much pleased with the courage and skill of the stranger, and wished to know his name and parentage. The young man said that his name was Orlando, and that he was the youngest son of Sir Rowland de Bois, who was now dead; but, when living, was a true subject and dear friend of the banished Duke.

When Frederick heard this all his liking for the young man changed into anger, and he left the place in a very ill humour. Rosalind, however, was delighted to hear that the gallant young man was the son of her father's old friend. She therefore spoke to him more kindly than before, and, taking a chain from her neck said, "Gentleman, wear this for me. I am out of favour with fortune, or I would give you a more valuable present."

When the ladies were alone, all Rosalind's talk was about Orlando, and Celia soon saw that her cousin had fallen in love with the handsome young wrestler. Shortly afterwards Duke Frederick entered the room. He was still angry, and his spite suddenly broke out against Rosalind. With angry words he bade her leave his palace and follow her father into banishment. Celia pleaded with him, but all in vain. Her father paid no heed to her, but angrily bade Rosalind begone.

Celia found that she could not prevail upon her father to let Rosalind remain with her, so she said that she would leave the palace too. She would go with her cousin, and together they would seek the banished Duke in the Forest of Arden. They would take with them the faithful Touchstone, who had served the banished duke as his jester or clown.

Before they set out, Celia thought it would be unsafe for two young ladies to travel together; so they decided that Rosalind, who was the taller of the two, should dress as a young countryman, and that Celia should attire herself as a country lass. They were to pass as brother and sister. Rosalind was to call herself Ganymede, and Celia chose the name of Aliena.

After many days they reached the forest; but both girls were worn out with fatigue, and Aliena declared that she could not go a step farther. Ganymede did his best to cheer her, but he too was faint and worn. At last they both sat by the roadside, the most downcast, weary, and unhappy pair that you ever beheld.

II

When they were thus resting by the roadside a countryman chanced to pass that way, and Ganymede tried to speak with a manly boldness. "Shepherd," she said, "I will give you thanks and gold if you will take us to a

ROSALIND, CELIA, AND TOUCHSTONE IN THE FOREST.
(*Sir John E. Millais, P.R.A.*)

place where we can rest in safety. This young maid, my sister, is much fatigued with travelling, and is faint for want of food."

The shepherd said that he was only a servant, and that his cottage was a poor place, but that they were welcome to all that was in it. The cottage was just going to be sold, and they might buy it, and the flock of sheep too, if they wished. Thereupon the two girls followed the man, and when they had refreshed themselves, they bought the house and the flock, and decided to remain in the cottage until they could learn in what part of the forest the Duke dwelt.

Now, quite unknown to the ladies, Orlando was in the forest too. His elder brother had always treated him harshly, because he was envious of his fine person and graceful manners. One day this wicked brother vowed that he would burn the chamber in which Orlando slept. He was overheard by an old and faithful servant who was devoted to Orlando because he resembled Sir Rowland, his former master and friend. This old man, whose name was Adam, warned Orlando of his danger, and begged him to leave the place that very night.

The faithful servant and his beloved master set out at once, and tramped on and on until they came to the Forest of Arden. By this time the old man was so weary that he cried, "Oh, my dear master, I die for want of food; I can go no farther." Orlando tried hard to cheer him, but when he saw how weak poor Adam was, he laid him tenderly under the shade of a tree and set off to seek food.

Suddenly he saw the Duke and his friends seated under a tree eating their dinner. Orlando was now desperate, and, drawing his sword, prepared to rob them of their meal. The banished nobleman, however, bade him sit down and help himself, and spoke so graciously to him that the young man was ashamed of his rudeness. He explained that he needed the food, not for himself but for his poor old servant, who was lying under a tree a mile or two away.

"Go, and bring him hither," said the Duke; and in a short time Orlando returned carrying Adam in his arms. Food and wine soon restored the old man, and when the Duke knew who Orlando was, he bade him join his company and live under his protection.

Now we must return to Ganymede and Aliena in their cottage. As they took their walks in the forest they were much surprised to see the name of Rosalind carved on the trees, and to find love verses to the same lady fastened to them. While they stood wondering at this strange discovery, who should come towards them but Orlando, wearing about his neck the chain which Rosalind had given him.

Of course, Orlando did not know that the handsome youth Ganymede was the fair lady Rosalind who had won his heart. Rosalind knew Orlando at once, and was overjoyed to meet him again, but she did not betray herself. She put on the forward manners of a pert youth, and began to make fun of the lover whose handiwork she saw about her. "If I could find this lover," she said, "I would give him some counsel, and would soon cure him of his love."

Then Orlando confessed that he was the lover, and begged the handsome youth to give him the good counsel which he talked of.

"WHO SHOULD COME TOWARDS THEM BUT ORLANDO."
(*See page 171.*)

One day, when walking in the forest, Ganymede met the Duke, and had some talk with him. The father did not know his daughter in male attire, but he was much interested in the pretty shepherd boy, and asked him his name and parentage. Ganymede answered pertly that his parentage was as good as the Duke's, and, seeing that the banished nobleman was well and happy, was content to put off further explanations for a few days longer.

One morning, when Orlando was on his way to visit Ganymede, he saw a man lying asleep on the ground with a large green snake twisted about his neck. When the snake saw Orlando it glided away amongst the bushes. The young man followed it, and discovered a lioness couching like a cat ready to spring upon the sleeping man as soon as he should wake. Lions, you know, will not feed upon a dead body, and this lioness was waiting to see the man stir, and thus show himself alive, before she sprang upon him.

Orlando looked at the man who was in such danger, and to his amazement found that it was the elder brother who had treated him so unkindly. For a moment he was tempted to leave his brother to the fate which he so well deserved, but soon his better nature overcame his anger, and, drawing his sword, he fell upon the lioness. She tore one of his arms with her sharp claws, but Orlando soon killed her.

Meanwhile the elder brother had awakened from sleep, and when he saw the brother whom he had so cruelly wronged risking his life to save the man who had wronged him, he was filled with shame and remorse, and begged Orlando's pardon for his misdeeds. Orlando gladly forgave him, and ever after the two brothers were the best of friends.

The wound in Orlando's arm bled so much that he found himself too weak to visit Ganymede. He therefore asked his brother to go to the cottage and tell the young shepherd what had befallen him.

III

Orlando's brother, who was named Oliver, immediately set out for the cottage, and introduced himself to the young shepherd and his sister. Then he told them all that had happened: how he lay sleeping in the forest, and how Orlando had delivered him, at the risk of his own life, from the fangs of the snake and the claws of the lioness. He further said that he was Orlando's elder brother, and that he had treated him most unkindly, and had even plotted to kill him, but that now he was full of shame, and was determined to make amends.

Then, in proof of his story, he showed them a bloodstained scarf, which had been used to bind up Orlando's wounds. At the sight of it Ganymede fainted, but soon recovered, and tried to pass off the weakness as a joke.

Oliver now returned to his brother, and told him how Ganymede had swooned on hearing that he had been wounded. He also confessed that he loved the fair shepherdess Aliena very dearly, and wished with all his heart to marry her. He believed that she loved him in return, and he proposed to live with her in the cottage as a shepherd, and to settle his estate and house at home upon the brother whom he had wronged. Orlando bade him go back to Aliena and persuade her to be married the very next day. Then he sighed, and said that it would be the greatest joy to him if he could be married to Rosalind at the same time.

At this moment Ganymede appeared, and Orlando told him of Oliver's love and of his own desire. Then Ganymede said that if Orlando really loved Rosalind as much as he professed to do, he should have his wish. He would make Rosalind appear in her own person on the morrow, and then Orlando would find that Rosalind was quite willing to marry him.

So next morning the Duke and his friends assembled to celebrate the double marriage. Oliver led Aliena by the hand into the presence of the Duke, and Orlando came with them; but Rosalind was nowhere to be seen, and Ganymede was missing.

When the Duke heard that it was his own daughter for whom they were waiting, he asked Orlando if he believed that the shepherd boy could really do what he had promised. Orlando replied that he knew not what to think; but as he was speaking Ganymede entered, and asked the Duke if he would consent to the marriage of Rosalind and Orlando. "That I would," said the Duke, "if I had kingdoms to give with her." Then Ganymede turned to Orlando and asked, "Would you marry her if I bring her here?" "That I would," said Orlando, "if I were king of many kingdoms."

Ganymede and Aliena then retired to their cottage, where the shepherd boy threw off his male attire, and being once more dressed in the garments of a woman quickly became Rosalind without the aid of magic. Aliena changed her country garb for her own rich clothes and just as quickly became the Lady Celia.

Soon Rosalind and Celia appeared in their own clothes, and the mystery was explained. Rosalind threw herself on her knees before her father and begged his blessing. She told him the whole story of her banishment, and how she had lived in the forest as a shepherd boy and passed off Celia as her sister.

Then the two couples were married amidst great rejoicing, and the wood rang with the sounds of merriment. As they sat down to dinner a messenger arrived with joyful news for the Duke. His kingdom had been restored to him, and he was free to return to his palace and once more rule his people.

This joyful news made the wedding-day still more happy. Celia, who had not a spark of envy in her nature, was full of joy at the good fortune which had restored Rosalind and the Duke to their rightful place. Though she was no longer a great heiress, she had the love of Oliver, and that was all that she desired.

And so this pretty story ends with wedding bells, wrongs righted, misdeeds forgiven, sins atoned for, and truth and loyalty rewarded. I am sure that the end of the story is just *As You Like It.*

Exercises

1. What is the difference between a tragedy and a comedy?
2. Explain how Rosalind and Orlando first met.
3. Write out a list of the chief persons in *As You Like It*, and in a few words, such as you would find on a playbill, describe each character. Begin thus:

   The Duke......................A ruler of one of the provinces of northern France.

   Frederick......................His younger brother.

   Rosalind......................etc.

4. Join the following pairs of sentences together by using *who, whose,* or *that*:

Once upon a time there was a duke; he had a younger
  brother.
The duke had a daughter; her name was Rosalind,
I saw a ship; it was sailing towards the land.
Orlando helped the old man; his name was Adam,

5. The Latin verb *scribo* means "I write." There are many English
   words which contain this word in the form of *scribe* or *script*.
   Write down six words containing *scribe* or *script*.
6. Describe the picture on page 169. How would you know this
   was not a West Indian scene, even if the characters were not
   there?

LESSON 28

RODNEY SAVES THE BRITISH WEST INDIES

WE have seen that during the eighteenth century England
and France were engaged in a long struggle for the possession of North America and India. The victories of Wolfe in
Canada and Olive in India decided the issue in favour of
England, and, at the end of what is known as the Seven Years'
War, the whole of North America from Labrador to Florida
passed into British possession. During the twelve years which
followed the peace, however, a strong feeling had been
growing up in the mother-country that the American colonies should be taxed, in order to raise money to pay off the
war debt, and to support a British army in America for their
future protection. To this the colonists strongly objected, on
the ground that, as they were not allowed to send members
to the British Parliament, Parliament had no right to impose
taxes on them.

As a result the New England States declared their independence, and war followed, in which the British armies were early defeated. The result of the reverse was a terrible blow to Britain, for France promptly made a treaty with America and prepared to take up arms against her old foe. Spain and Holland followed suit, and Britain was thus practically isolated. The French navy contributed in no small measure to the success of the American colonists, as by the skilful disposition of his fleet their admiral cut off the British troops from their supplies and prevented their retreat by sea. Thus did France avenge herself for the loss of Canada, and, moreover, she then endeavoured to win back in the West Indies what she had lost there earlier in the century.

The French admiral, Count de Grasse, sailed down the islands with the intention of sweeping out the British altogether. His efforts in this direction were so far successful, that within a very short space of time Jamaica, Barbados, and Antigua alone remained to us of our old West Indian colonies, while St. Lucia was the only island among our more recent possessions over which our flag still floated.

Fortunately for us, Britain, as is her wont, found her saviour in her hour of need, when Admiral Lord Rodney was sent out to command our fleet in the West Indies, sped by the parting words of the Lord of the Admiralty: "The fate of this empire is in your hands, and I have no wish that it should be in any other." How this confidence was justified can be judged from the story of Rodney's brilliant victory over Count de Grasse in the "Battle of the Saints" off Dominica on the memorable 12th of April, 1782.

Spain and France intended to join hands at Cap François, where there would be assembled an overpowering fleet of fifty ships of the line, and twenty thousand troops. To prevent this junction, Rodney, who had previously seen service in the Caribbean, again left England, and with a squadron of twelve ships made for Barbados. On 25th February Commodore Hood, who had already by clever seamanship more than held his own against De Grasse, joined Rodney off Antigua, bringing the latter's strength up to

Admiral Lord Rodney.

thirty-four ships of the line, a force which was afterwards, by fresh arrivals, increased to thirty-seven.

During the entire month of March, Rodney lay at St. Lucia in the spacious Gros Islet Bay, keeping, by means of his frigates, a watchful eye on De Grasse at Martinique. The latter had now at his disposal thirty-three ships of the line, and two 50-gun ships. Day and night the thirty miles of sea which separated the two fleets was patrolled by Rodney's chain of frigates, ever repeating from end to end of their line signals by flag or lamp, reporting to their chief each movement of the enemy. Not till the 5th of April came the signal that the French were on the move, and were then actually leaving port, their evident intention being to make a desperate effort to join with the Spanish fleet at San Domingo. Rodney at once got under way. By afternoon his leading frigates were in sight of the French fleet.

At daybreak on the 9th Rodney was abreast of Dominica, but becalmed; to the north and east of him were seen the French, somewhat scattered owing to the light and baffling winds. Part of their fleet, however, had caught the sea breeze, and gradually others, hitherto becalmed, gaining steerage-way, were enabled to draw up. At the same time the English van under Hood felt the breeze, and made for two French vessels isolated from the rest of their force. To save these De Grasse ordered his foremost ships to bear down and engage.

The action began at 9 a.m., eight or nine of the English ships opposed by fifteen French. Gradually, however, as the breeze waxed in power the two fleets were able to concentrate their strength, with the exception of the English rear, which still lay helplessly becalmed. But though the French were to windward, thus having the choice of bringing on or avoiding battle, they kept their distance, and no general action resulted. Indeed, before 2 p.m. the enemy, seeing the whole British fleet now coming up, ceased firing and hauled off.

No great damage was done; two English ships were disabled, but were able to repair their damages without leaving the fleet; one French vessel was so badly mauled that she was obliged to make for port. It is not easy to see why De Grasse did not that day work irreparable damage on the English, for at no time were more than twenty

English ships available to oppose the thirty-three French, which had the breeze.

Until the 12th of April Rodney continued to toil after the French fleet, but without ever being able to gain on them; on the contrary, the enemy gradually but surely increased their distance. On the night of the 10th two French vessels came into collision, and from that little circumstance arose disaster to their whole force. The injuries sustained by one of them, the *Zélé*, so delayed her and a consort that De Grasse was forced to change his course in order to save them, thus greatly reducing the distance between the two fleets. Next evening the same vessel, the *Zélé*, was again in collision, this time with De Grasse's flagship, the *Ville de Paris,* and at daybreak on the 12th the *Zélé*, in tow, was seen by the English making for Basse Terre, in Guadeloupe. Rodney at once signalled to four of his ships to overhaul her, in the hope that De Grasse would be forced again to come to her assistance, and that it would consequently be impossible for him longer to avoid a general action.

All happened as Rodney desired. To save the *Zélé*, De Grasse bore down, and slowly in the light breeze the two fleets crept nearer to each other. At first they were merely passing each other on different tacks, each vessel as opportunity offered bringing her guns to bear. Then came a sudden shift of wind, a gap in the French line, and Rodney's opportunity.

"Rodney, in the *Formidable,* was at this time just drawing up with the fourth ship astern of De Grasse's flag. Luffing to the new wind, he passed through the French line, followed by the five ships next astern of him, while nearly at the same moment, and from the same causes,

"HE PASSED THROUGH THE FRENCH LINE." (*See page 181.*)

his sixth astern led through the interval abreast of him, followed by the whole English rear."[*]

The French line of battle was broken in two places and from that moment disaster hurried on the heels of disaster, culminating in the capture, by Hood in the *Barfleur,* of De Grasse's flagship, the powerful *Ville de Paris,* the largest ship in the French navy. Five other ships of the line were taken and one sunk, and a few days later two more ships of the line and two frigates were captured by Hood. The British fleet was becalmed off Guadeloupe, and the crippled remains of the French fleet managed to reach Cap François under M. de Bougainville.

The West Indies were saved; the victory ruined the naval power of France and put an end to all her hopes of establishing an empire on this side of the Atlantic. It was a momentous victory, and of all our many naval triumphs, the "Battle of the Saints" was possibly exceeded by Trafalgar alone.

EXERCISES

1. Why do you think the battle was named the "Battle of the Saints"? Study the north-west of Dominica in your atlas.
2. How has the name of one of the French leaders been perpetuated throughout the West Indies?
3. Draw a plan of the battle, showing how Rodney broke through the French line.
4. Two large British battleships, built in 1927, were named the *Nelson* and the *Rodney.* Why were these names chosen for our latest and most powerful battleships? Other British

---

[*] Mahan, *Influence of Sea Power.*

warships are the *Benbow,* the *Hood,* and the *Vernon.* Why were they given these names?

5. Study the picture on page 182. Which of the ships is British and which French? How do you know?

6. Rodney had long regarded St. Lucia as an ideal naval base. Why did it give him great advantages while waiting for the French? (Use your atlas in answering this question.)

LESSON 29

INSECT PESTS—I

INSECT PESTS OF CROPS

Note to Teacher.—Before reading this chapter, Lesson 2 in Book III. should be revised, and a lesson given on Insects: (1) those which pass through the four stages of egg, larva, pupa, and adult, such as moths, butterflies, beetles, flies, mosquitoes, bees, wasps, and ants; and (2) those which, when hatched from the egg, have a general resemblance to the adult, such as plant bugs, cotton stainers, scale insects, grasshoppers, crickets, and cockroaches. (See Watts' *Nature Teaching.*)

WE have seen in previous lessons that insects are the most numerous of all the forms of animal life—so numerous, in fact, that but for their natural enemies, such as birds, lizards, frogs, and toads, and also other insects, they might increase so rapidly as to destroy our crops altogether. Even as it is they are very formidable enemies of the planter, who is put to considerable expense and labour in controlling those species which infest his plantations.

In this lesson, therefore, we will learn something of the more common pests of our staple West Indian crops. Some insects are pests of more than one crop, as, for example, the moth-borer, which attacks both sugar-cane and Indian corn or maize; or the cotton boll worm, which is a serious pest of both cotton and corn. It must be remembered, too, that while insects may be common pests of crops in certain islands, in others

Moth-borer (caterpillar).

the crops may be quite immune from their attacks; the froghopper, which is a serious pest of sugar-cane in Trinidad and Grenada, is unknown in the neighbouring island of Barbados, where strict regulations have been made by the Government to prevent its importation through the medium of cane, soil, or packing materials.

Your teacher will tell you which of the insects referred to in this lesson are pests in your own colony.

Sugar-cane.—One of the most serious of the pests of sugar-cane in the West Indies is the *moth-borer,* which lays its flat scale-like eggs in clusters on the leaves of the cane. The larva or caterpillar which emerges from the egg travels down the leaf to its base, and bores its way into the stem.

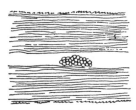

Eggs of Moth-borer.

The remaining stages of its life history, up to the coming of the moth, are spent in the tunnel it has made. When the moth emerges it lays more eggs, and the process is repeated. The numerous tunnels thus made in the stem result in considerable injury to the cane.

Another common pest of the sugar-cane is the *weevil-borer,* which, unlike the moth-borer, deposits its eggs in the cane itself in cut or broken parts or in the soft part above the hard joints. When the larva, which is a small white grub, appears, it tunnels into the cane, where it makes a rough cocoon from the fibres of the stem. After the pupal

stage has passed, the adult or fully developed insect—the beetle—emerges. Its egg-laying continues for some time, so that much damage may be done on an estate where this pest gains a foothold and remains unchecked for even a short space of time.

Cocoon of Weevil-borer.

There are other borers, such as the *root-borer,* common in certain Parts of Barbados, and the *shot-borer.*

The *cane fly* lives on the leaves and stems of sugar-cane, obtaining its food by sucking the juices of its host. The female lays its eggs in slits which it makes in the tissues of the leaf. As black fungus grows on the canes whenever these insects are present in large numbers, it was first known as "black blight."

In St. Kitts especially, the *grasshopper* is a formidable pest of sugar-cane. The insect eats the leaves, particularly those of young canes. *White ants* or termites, which do considerable damage to the timber of buildings, also attack ripening canes and eat the inner part of the stem.

In Trinidad and several other colonies the growing canes are subject at intervals to serious damage in the form of a browning and drying up of the leaves and a decay of the root system, which gives an appearance as if the field had been scorched by fire. This was originally known as "blight," but is now known to be caused by an insect called the *froghopper*. This pest lives on and sucks the juices of the leaves in its winged adult stage, and on the roots, where it lives in its young or nymph stage, surrounded by a peculiar white froth.

Cacao.—The cacao planter also has numerous insect enemies, but perhaps the most dangerous of all is the cacao beetle, which lays its eggs in the bark of the tree, in small pits made by itself. The grubs bore under the bark, and the pupæ lie there in the tunnels until they become adult beetles. Their presence is often shown by the dry shrunken appearance of the bark.

Froghopper: natural size and enlarged.

Another common pest of cacao is a small insect, known by the name *cacao thrips,* which attacks the leaves and

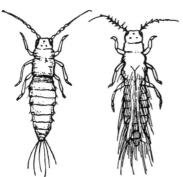

Cacao Thrips: young insect (*left*), and adult (*right*).

pods. Like the cane fly, the female lays its eggs in little slits which it cuts in the tissues of the plant. The young insect may be detected by the bright red band across its abdomen, whilst the adult can be recognized by its wings, which are fringed with long delicate hairs. The cacao is injured by the actual feeding of the thrips, whose mouth is specially adapted for piercing the surface and sucking the juice from beneath. Discoloration is produced on the pods where the insects have attacked them.

In some islands, including St. Lucia and St. Vincent, a

species of *beetle* occasionally attacks cacao trees by eating the leaves; in places, too, where the crop is growing on lands previously under sugar, the root-borer of the sugar-cane has been known as a pest.

Cacao Beetle and Larva.

Cotton.—This crop appears to be the favourite among insects, judging by the number of different kinds which attack it.

The *cotton worm* has been known ever since cotton has been cultivated in the West Indies, and in some of the islands, notably Barbados, Montserrat, Antigua, Nevis, and St. Kitts, the cotton fields have at times been laid bare by the ravages of this pest, which feeds upon the leaves during its caterpillar stage. It

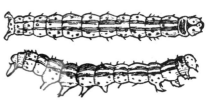

Cotton-worm Larva (enlarged), back view and side view.

lays its eggs on the under side of the tender leaves at the growing tips of the plant. You can see what they look like from the picture, but it must be remembered that in reality they are much smaller.

The larva which issues from the egg of the cotton worm is a green caterpillar about one and a half inches long, with a fine bluish white line running along the middle of its back, bordered on either side by a broad green band, and each of these in turn by one of yellowish green. The caterpillar changes into the pupa within a portion of folded leaf secured by means of a few silken threads, which forms a kind of cocoon. From this the adult insect, a small olive-grey moth, appears. The

Eggs of Cotton Worm (much enlarged).

females lay about 300 eggs, so that the pest would increase very rapidly but for its own natural enemies, such as birds, toads, lizards, ground-beetles, and wild bees or Jack Spaniards.

Cotton stainers are small insects with mouths specially adapted for sucking the juices of plants. They lay their

Cotton Stainer.

eggs in the opening cotton bolls or on the ground beneath the plant. You can see from the picture, which is three times the natural size, what the insect looks like. There are many species of cotton stainers, this one being red in colour with black and white markings on its wings. All the kinds are alike in habit: they feed on the growing cotton bolls, on the seed, and on the leaf and tender stems of the plant.

The *cotton boll worm*, which you can see attacking a cotton boll in the picture on next page, is an insect which is found in most temperate and tropical parts of the world. It does not confine its attacks to the cotton plant,

but feeds and thrives on many plants, such as corn, tobacco, peas, and beans, generally preferring the fruit to the leaves. The caterpillar burrows into the cotton bolls and completely destroys their interior.

Cotton Boll Worm attacking a Cotton Boll.

Among other pests of cotton are the *flower-bud maggot,* the *leaf-blister mite,* the *corn-ear worm,* the *red maggot,* the *cotton aphis,* the *cut worm,* the *red spider,* the *boll weevil,* and both black and white *scale insects.*

Coconuts.—These trees are subject to the attacks of several species of pests, the chief of which are *scale insects,* which are found on the older leaves, where enormous numbers are often seen closely crowded together. The leaves when badly attacked often have a yellowish or dried-up appearance.

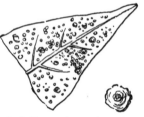

Scale Insects (one enlarged).

Another common enemy of the coconut is the *white fly,* which has been considered largely responsible for the decrease in the number of coconut trees on the leeward side of Barbados. This pest is often found working along with scale insects, and its colonies may be detected by the presence of fine wax threads on the leaves.

Other Crops.—In addition to those mentioned, other crops are subject to attacks of their particular enemies. The citrus fruits are attacked by scale insects, the lantern bug, the white fly, bark borers, fruit flies, and the rust mite; arrowroot by the arrowroot worm; tobacco by the tobacco worm and the flea beetle; sweet potatoes by the scarabee or Jacobs, the sweet-potato worm, the weevil, thrips, and the red spider; nutmegs by mealy shield scale; bananas by white flies and the banana borer; yams by scale insects; and grass by the mole cricket.

Mole Cricket.

You will learn more of those pests which are common in your particular colony, in your Nature Study lessons, when your teacher will also tell you how they are controlled by their own natural enemies and by artificial means adopted by planters and others.

EXERCISES

1. Make a list of all the colours mentioned in this lesson. How many are there?
2. How could you classify insects according to the stages through which they pass in their life history? Give examples in each class.

3. How many insect pests are referred to? Complete the table, showing their names and the plants which they infest.

Insect Pests.	Crops they attack.
moth-borer ⎰	sugar-cane Indian corn
weevil-borer	sugar-cane
root-borer	....
....	....
.... etc.	.... etc.

4. Make drawings of a cacao thrips, a cotton stainer, and a mole cricket.

5. Form sentences of your own containing these words:

previous	regulations	recognized
adult	immune	preferring
numerous	originally	artificial
formidable	decay	detected

6. Name the common insect pests of your own colony. Say what you can about them.

7. Give the *opposites* of the following:

natural	strict	emerges
increase	rapidly	remembered
numerous	adult	common
presence	delicate	inner

LESSON 30

THE VALUE OF HYGIENE

HYGIENE, or the science of keeping well, so called from the Greek name of the goddess of health, teaches us how to keep healthy by preventing sickness or disease. You have seen in previous lessons that in order that people may run the fewest possible risks of contracting diseases, *everything must be made as clean as possible*—in fact, it may almost be said that "sanitation is cleanliness."

The food you eat must be clean; the water you drink and cook with, and wash in, must be clean; the clothes you wear, and the rooms you live in, must be clean; the very air you breathe must be clean, if your bodies are to be free from disease, for disease may lurk in all these—food, water, clothing, dwellings, air—though it can only flourish when they are unclean.

You have learned, too, that in addition to cleanliness there are certain other things that are essential to health. These are nutrition, fresh air, exercise, rest, and warmth, and a knowledge of the requirements of our bodies in these respects is equally important. Hygiene, therefore, must include the proper use of these essentials.

Closely related to these is the care of the special senses, of sight and hearing, and of the mind, for it is through these faculties that we are able to adjust our bodies to the world in which we live.

It is thus easy to realize that hygiene is largely a personal and individual affair, which concerns each one of us, and that our own good health depends principally upon our own individual actions. An important point to remember, too, is that the *knowledge* of what we should do is of little value unless we *make use* of it in our daily life. To learn arithmetic or writing is of no advantage to you unless you put your knowledge into practice. Similarly, you might learn by heart all the lessons on Hygiene in these Readers, and be able to say them off "word perfect," but this would not make you or your country any healthier, unless you practise what you have learned.

Hundreds of years ago people thought that sickness was either caused by "the will of Providence" or "the work of the Devil," or "the result of witch craft." Even to-day, in countries where there are few schools and where the people are uneducated, they still believe these things; but in places, such as the West Indies, where children learn hygiene in schools, we know better, and through this knowledge we are able to reap the advantage of the great work which doctors have been doing in the last century or so, in finding out the *causes* of ill-health. By learning how to avoid diseases, and by obtaining proper treatment if we are attacked by them, each of us can not only enjoy a more healthy life, but can also do his share towards making his country more healthy for others to live in.

Much good work in this direction is done by the public health officers and sanitary inspectors, and it is very necessary that we should give them all possible assistance. Two examples of the work of the Public Health Service in this part of the world will show how valuable are the activities of its officers. For many years attempts had been made to construct the Panama Canal across the narrow isthmus of Central America, but they all resulted in failure, through the ravages of yellow fever among the labourers. It was at last discovered that this disease is carried from person to person by a certain kind of mosquito, and the engineers called in the help of the doctors to make the country as free from disease as possible by taking steps to kill the mosquitoes, and by providing suitable dwellings and hospitals. Then the labourers remained healthy, and the wonderful canal joining the Atlantic and Pacific oceans was completed.

In Havana, the capital of Cuba, for many years earlier than this, yellow fever was also common, and the disease wrought much havoc among the inhabitants. Although at that time the mosquito was suspected to be the carrier of the disease, it was not definitely known to be so until some brave doctors voluntarily risked their lives by allowing themselves to be bitten by a mosquito which had previously bitten a person suffering from yellow fever. From these and other experiments it was proved that the mosquito was really the carrier, and the people started a campaign to exterminate this dangerous insect. In one year Havana was freed from yellow fever.

Hygiene not only teaches us how to keep free from disease, but also how to get the best enjoyment and use out of life. A great many years ago a Roman philosopher wrote: "Life is not existence, but health." This saying will always remain true, for without health it is impossible to obtain the fullest happiness and pleasure from life.

We are so accustomed to hear of sickness among relatives and friends that we have unfortunately got into the habit of thinking of health merely as the absence of disease. This is an entirely wrong idea; health is much more than this—it is really something which we can attain, not just the state when disease is absent. Good health consists of keeping our bodies and minds in the best possible condition.

We know that if we wish to get the best results from anything, it is a good rule to ascertain carefully what that thing can do and the way in which it should be used. Driving at fifty miles an hour a machine that is built to go at twenty miles an hour is very unwise. Stresses and strains are set up, with dire results to the machine itself.

Although we apply this rule to the things we use in our games and in our work, we frequently disregard it in the case of our bodies, and forget that if we wish to keep fit and well we must try to learn something of the needs and capacities of our bodies. The human body is the most wonderful machine in existence, on account of its power to adapt itself to varying conditions and circumstances, but even in the case of strong and robust persons there are limits beyond which play, exercise, or work will cause damage.

Our instincts and feelings are not always safe guides. We may feel tired at the end of the school day, and yet need exercise; we may feel energetic and excited after games, and yet need rest. One of the important lessons of hygiene is to teach ourselves control and restraint; these help us to appreciate the needs and rights of others, and are also necessary for a normal life.

The road to health and fitness is not through any one form of exercise or any special diet. Its sound foundation is best built by adopting the broad principle of avoiding extremes and excesses, and taking the common-sense middle course of developing clean and moderate health habits both of body and mind.

EXERCISES

1. What is "hygiene"? Why do we have hygiene lessons in school?
2. What are the essentials for good health?
3. Explain why hygiene is largely a personal and individual matter.
4. A person who takes alcoholic drink to excess does harm to his body and mind, as the muscles of the heart and body generally are weakened, and the functions of the brain are depressed. Excess in other directions can be equally harmful. Show how this is so with regard to eating, sleeping, exercise, work, and play.
5. Why are sanitary inspectors employed? What is their work? Are they our friends or enemies? Why?

LESSON 31

PICTURE LESSONS—VI

SALISBURY CATHEDRAL

JOHN CONSTABLE was a fine painter of English cultivated scenery, as we saw from his picture of "The Hay Wain" in Book IV. Often, too, he drew and painted the magnificent cathedral of Salisbury (as shown on page 199). Let us see how he seems to have composed this particular picture.

If he had merely filled the canvas with the outline of the cathedral, *that* would have given us quite a good likeness, but then it would not have been artistic. So he throws it back into the distance, and to do this more effectually he makes the foreground much darker and richer in colour than the rest. Compare the fine dark browns on the ground and in the trunks of the trees with the yellow-green in the sunshine, and the fresh yellow-greens in the trees that lie farther back.

Now this difference between sunlight and shadow would do much to make a fine picture. Constable does more than this to keep the eye and mind centred upon the cathedral. He places, on either side of its spire, gracefully bending trees which contrast with the many upright lines in the building; for contrast (such as between light and dark, or straight and curved) is one of the most common means to aid the artist in composing a picture.

Next he sweeps some fine curves through the outlying trees down through the little tree in the foreground, then along the backs of the cows, and so on through the trunk on the right, and into the clouds. In the centre of all this "movement" the cathedral stands with increased dignity and beauty.

All these curves, however, lead the eye *round* the building rather than directly to it, so Constable has thrust out two branches, one on either side of the tree trunk in the middle of the picture, in such a way as to lead the eye at once to the spire.

You can find out other ways in which he binds the parts together. There is, for instance, the path that, leading from the front, goes in a curved line (which you can mark by the people walking on it in the distance) towards the base of the steeple.

SALISBURY CATHEDRAL. (*John Constable.*)

Then, again, two little figures that stand out strongly because the artist has painted them in strong red, blue, and white, are on this path. Both look towards the cathedral, to which the man points.

So that, as our eyes wander about the picture, they are brought back again to the cathedral by the most skilful use of pictorial "composition."

EXERCISE

Write a paragraph describing, in your own words, what you can see in Constable's picture.

LESSON 32

DESCRIPTIVE EXTRACTS—II

Introduction.—The following descriptions are taken from *The English in the West Indies, or the Bow of Ulysses,* by J. A. Froude, who visited the West Indian Islands in 1887 in order to increase his acquaintance with the condition of the then British colonies. Froude had a great reputation as a writer of English, and these extracts, written when he was a man of close on seventy, are a rare testimony to his keenness of observation and his enthusiasm for things beautiful.

(*a*) IN BARBADOS

I STARTED in the early morning, before the sun was above the trees. The road followed the line of the shore. Originally, I believe, Barbados was like the Antilles, covered with forest. In the interior little remains save cabbage palms and detached clumps of mangy-looking mahogany trees. The forest is gone, and human beings have taken the place of it.

For ten miles I was driving through a string of straggling villages, each cottage or cabin having its small vegetable garden and clump of plantains. Being on the western or sheltered side of the island, the sea was smooth and edged with mangrove, through which at occasional openings we saw the shining water and the white coral beach and fishing-boats either drawn up upon it or anchored outside with their sails up.

Trees had been planted for shade among the houses. There were village greens with great silk-cotton trees, banyans and acacias, mangoes and oranges, and shad-docks with their large fruit glowing among the leaves like great golden melons. The people swarmed, children tumbling about half naked, so like each other that one wondered whether their mothers knew their own from their neighbours'; the fishermen's wives selling flying-fish, of which there are infinite numbers.

It was an innocent, pretty scene. One missed green fields with cows upon them. Guinea grass, which is all that they have, makes excellent fodder, but is ugly to look at; and is cut and carried, not eaten where it grows. Of animal life there were innumerable donkeys, infinite poultry, and pigs, familiar enough, but not allowed a free entry into the cabins as in Ireland.

Of birds there was not any great variety. The humming-birds preferred less populated quarters. There were small varieties of finches and sparrows and buntings, winged atoms without beauty of form or colour; there were a few wild pigeons; but the prevailing figure was the Barbadian crow, a little black fellow, who gets his living upon worms and insects and parasites, and so tame that he would perch upon a boy's head if he saw a chance of anything eatable there.

The women in Barbados imitate English ladies in their dress; but no dress can conceal the grace of their forms when they are young. They work harder than the men, and are used as beasts of burden to fetch and carry, but they carry their loads on their heads, and thus from childhood have to stand upright with the neck straight and firm. They do not spoil their shapes with stays, or their walk with high-heeled shoes. They plant their feet firmly on the ground. Every movement is elastic and rounded, and the grace of body gives, or seems to give, grace also to the eyes and expression.

After keeping by the sea for an hour we turned inland, and at the foot of a steep hill we met my host, who transferred me to his own carriage. We had still four or five miles to go through cane fields and among sugar mills. At the end of them we came to a grand avenue of cabbage palms, a hundred or a hundred and twenty feet high.

How their slim stems with their dense coronet of leaves survive a hurricane is one of the West Indian marvels. They escape destruction by the elasticity with which they yield to it. The branches, which in a calm stand out symmetrically, forming a circle of which the stem is the exact centre, bend round before a violent wind, are pressed close together, and stream out horizontally like a horse's tail.

(b) A PEEP AT JAMAICA

Arrangements were made for amusements and expeditions in which I was invited to join—which were got up, perhaps, for my own entertainment. I was to be taken to the sights of the neighbourhood; I was to see this; I was to see that; above all, I must see the Peak of the Blue Mountains. The peak itself I could see better from below, for there it stood, never moving, between seven and eight thousand feet high. But I had mountain riding enough, and was allowed to plead my age and infirmities. It was finally arranged that I should be driven the next day to Castleton, seventeen miles over a mountain pass, to see the Botanical Gardens.

Accordingly, early on the following morning we set off, two carriages full of us. The road was as good as all roads in Jamaica, and more cannot be said in their favour. Forest trees made a roof over our heads as we climbed to the crest of the ridge. Thence we descended the side of a long valley, a stream running below us, which gradually grew into a river.

We passed through all varieties of cultivation. On the high ground there was a large sugar plantation; in the alluvial meadows on the river-side were tobacco fields, cleanly and carefully kept, belonging to my Spanish friend in Kingston, and only too rich in leaves. There were sago too, and ginger, and tamarinds, and cocoa, and coffee, and coconut palms.

On the hillsides were the garden farms of the peasants, which were something to see and remember. They receive from the Government at an almost nominal rent an acre or two of uncleared forest. To this, as the first step, they set light; at twenty different spots we saw fires blazing. To clear an acre they waste timber on half a dozen. They plant their yams and sweet potatoes among the ashes, and grow crops of these till the soil is exhausted. Then they move on to another, which they treat with the same recklessness, leaving the first to go back to scrub. Since the Chinaman burnt his house to roast his pig, such waste was never seen.

The male proprietors were lounging about smoking. Their wives, as it was market-day, were tramping into Kingston with their baskets on their heads. We met them literally in thousands, all merry and light-hearted, their little ones with their little baskets trudging at their side.

We reached Castleton at last. It was in a hot, damp valley. The gardens slightly disappointed me; my expectations had been too much raised at Trinidad. There were lovely flowers, of course, and curious plants and trees. Every known palm is growing there. They try hard to grow roses, and they say that they succeed. The roses were not in flower, and I could not judge.

Wild nature also was luxuriantly beautiful. We picnicked by the river, which here is a full rushing stream with pools that would have held a salmon, and which did hold abundant mullet. We found a bower formed by a twisted vine, so thick that neither sun nor rain could penetrate the roof.

The floor was of shining shingle, and the air breathed cool from off the water. It was a spot which nymph or naiad may haunt hereafter, when nymphs are born again in the new era; and we were a pleasant party of human beings, lying about under the shade upon the pebbles.

I remember no more of the gardens except that I saw a mongoose stalking a flock of turkeys. The young ones and their mother gathered together and showed fight. The old cock, after the manner of the male animal, seemed chiefly anxious for his own skin, though a little ashamed at the same time, as if conscious that more was expected of him. On the way back we met the returning stream of women and children, loaded heavily as before and with the same elastic step.

(c) DOMINICA

There was much to be seen in Dominica of the sort which travellers go in search of. There was the hot sulphur spring in the mountains; there was the hot lake; there was another volcanic crater, a hollow in the centre of the island now filled with water and surrounded with forest; there were the Caribs, some thirty families of them living among thickets, through which paths must be cut before we could reach them. We could undertake nothing till Captain Churchill* could ride again. Distant expeditions can only be attempted on horses. They are bred to the work. They climb like cats, and step out safely where a fall or a twisted ankle would be the probable consequence of attempting to go on foot. Meanwhile Roseau itself was to be seen and the immediate neighbourhood.

My first night was disturbed by unfamiliar noises and strange imaginations. I escaped mosquitoes through the care of the black fairies. But mosquito curtains will not keep out sounds, and when the fireflies had put out their lights there began the singular chorus of tropical midnight. Frogs, lizards, bats, croaked, sang, and whistled with no intermission, careless whether they were in discord or harmony. The palm branches outside my window swayed in the land breeze, and the dry branches rustled crisply, as if they were plates of silver.

At intervals came cataracts of rain, and above all the rest the deep boom of the cathedral bell tolling out the hours like a note of the Old World. The Catholic clergy had brought the bells with them as they had brought their faith into these new lands. Towards morning I heard the tinkle of the bell of the convent adjoining the garden calling the nuns to matins. Happily in the tropics hot nights do

* The Administrator at that time.

not imply an early dawn. The darkness lingers late, sleep comes at last, and drowns our fancies in forgetfulness.

The swimming bath was immediately under my room. I ventured into it with some trepidation. The basement story in most West Indian houses is open, to allow the air free passage under them. The space thus left vacant is used for lumber and rubbish, and, if scorpions or snakes are in the neighbourhood, is the place where one would look for them. There the bath was. I had been advised to be careful, and as it was dark this was not easy. The fear, however, was worse than the reality. Awkward encounters do happen if one is long in these countries; but they are rare, and seldom befall the accidental visitor; and the plunge into fresh water is so delicious that one is willing to risk the chance.

I wandered out as soon as the sun was over the horizon. The cool of the morning is the time to see the people. The market girls were streaming into the town with their baskets of vegetables on their heads. The fishing-boats were out again on the bay. From the cathedral I roamed through the streets of Roseau; they had been well laid out; the streets themselves, and the roads leading to them from the country, had been carefully paved, and spoke of a time when the town had been full of life and vigour. But the grass was growing between the stones, and the houses generally were dilapidated. A few massive stone buildings there were, on which time and rain had made no impression.

In Roseau, as in most other towns, the most interesting spot is the market. There you see the produce of the soil;

there you see the people that produce it; and you see them, not on show, as in church on Sundays, but in their active working condition.

The market-place at Roseau is a large square court close to the sea, well paved, surrounded by warehouses, and luxuriantly shaded by large overhanging trees. Under these trees were hundreds of women, young and old, with their fish and fowls, and fruit and bread, their yams and sweet potatoes, their oranges and limes and plantains. They had walked in from the country five or ten miles before sunrise with their loaded baskets on their heads. They would walk back at night with flour or salt-fish, or oil, or whatever they happened to want. I did not see a single sullen face among them. They moved with the lightness and elasticity of leopards. I thought that I had never seen in any drawing-room in London so many perfectly graceful forms.

From the market I stepped back upon the quay, where I had the luck to witness a novel form of fishing, the most singular I have ever fallen in with. I have mentioned the herring-sized white fish which come in upon the shores of the island. They travel, as most small fish do, in enormous shoals, and keep, I suppose, in the shallow waters to avoid the king-fish and bonitos, who are good judges in their way, and find these small creatures exceptionally excellent.

The wooden pier ran out perhaps a hundred and fifty feet into the sea. It was a platform standing on piles, with openings in several places from which stairs led down to landing-stages. The depth at the extremity was about five fathoms. There is little or no tide, the difference between high water and low being not more than a couple of feet. Looking down the staircases, I saw among the piles in the brilliantly clear-water unnumbered thousands of the fish which I have described.

The fishermen had carried a long net round the pier from shore to shore, completely enclosing it. The fish were shut in, and had no means of escape except at the shore end, where boys were busy driving them back with stones; but how the net was to be drawn among the piles, or what was to be done next, I was curious to learn.

I was not left long to conjecture. A circular bag net was produced, made of fine strong thread, coloured a light green, and almost invisible in the sea. When it was spread, one side could be left open and could be closed at will by a running line from above. This net was let carefully down between the piles, and was immediately swollen out by the current which runs along the coast into a deep bay.

Two young fellows then dived; one saw them swimming about under water like sharks, hunting the fish before them as a dog would hunt a flock of sheep. Their companions, who were watching from the platform, waited till they saw as many driven into the purse of the inner net as they could trust the meshes to bear the weight of. The cord was then drawn. The net was closed. Net and all that it contained were hoisted into a boat, carried ashore and emptied. The net itself was then brought back and spread again for a fresh haul.

In this way I saw as many fish caught as would have filled a large cart. The contrivance, I believe, is one more inheritance from the Caribs, whom Labat describes as doing something of a similar kind.

JAMES ANTHONY FROUDE.

EXERCISES

1. What does Froude describe as a West Indian marvel?
2. In extract (b) there is a description which you have previously read in verse. What is the subject of the description, and in what poem have you read it?
3. Have you heard the story of the Chinaman who discovered the fact that roast pig was delicious? If not, perhaps your teacher will tell it to you; it is found in the *Essays of Elia*, by Charles Lamb.
4. What methods of fishing other than the one described do you know of? Which method is most common in your colony?
5. Describe a journey in your own island, with "In Barbados" as a model.
6. Make a list of all the living things mentioned in the lesson. Classify them as human beings, birds, animals (mammals), plants, fishes, reptiles, etc. Which class contains the most names in your list?
7. Make sentences of your own containing these words:

penetrate	survive
immediately	awkward
neighbourhood	unnumbered
abundant	contrivance
elastic	hoisted
grace	extremity

LESSON 33

"KING JOHN"

Introduction.—The following scene is from Shakespeare's play of *King John.* John seized the English throne after the death of his brother, Richard I. He is referred to in *Ivanhoe* in Lesson 19. The rightful heir to the throne was young Arthur, the son of John's elder brother Geoffrey. King John therefore sent his young nephew as a prisoner to a castle in England, placing him under the strict watch of one of his lords, named Hubert de Burgh. He had already declared to Hubert that he should have no rest until the boy's life had been taken; but, in the first place, he commanded Hubert to put out his eyes with red-hot irons. The scene describes Hubert attempting to carry out this terrible deed. Arthur pleads so pathetically for protection, that Hubert finally is moved to pity. He orders the attendants to go away, and promises that the boy's eyes shall not be put out, but he adds, "Your uncle must not know but you are dead." A sad and tragic end, however, was yet in store for poor Arthur. Hoping to escape from his cruel uncle to some safe place of hiding, he jumped from the castle wall, but was so terribly injured by the fall that he died.

ACT IV

SCENE I

A Room in a Castle.

[*Enter Hubert and two Attendants.*]

Hubert. Heat me these irons hot; and look thou stand
Within the arras: when I strike my foot
Upon the bosom of the ground, rush forth

And bind the boy that you will find with me
Fast to the chair. Be heedful; hence, and watch.

    Attendant. I hope your warrant will bear out the deed.
    Hubert. Uncleanly scruples! fear not you; look to't.
                           [Exeunt Attendants.]
Young lad, come forth; I have to speak with you.
                 [Enter Arthur.]
    Arthur. Good morrow, Hubert.
    Hubert.   Good morrow, little prince.
    Arthur. As little prince, having so great a title
To be more prince, as may be. You are sad.
    Hubert. Indeed, I have been merrier.
    Arthur.   Mercy on me!
Methinks nobody should be sad but I;
Yet, I remember, when I was in France,
Young gentlemen would be as sad as night,
Only for wantonness. By my Christendom,
So I were out of prison and kept sheep,
I should be as merry as the day is long;
And so I should be here, but that I doubt
My uncle practises more harm to me;
He is afraid of me and I of him.
Is it my fault that I was Geoffrey's son?
No, indeed, is't not; and I would to heaven
I were your son, so you would love me, Hubert.
    Hubert [*aside*]. If I talk to him, with his innocent prate
He will awake my mercy which lies dead;
Therefore I will be sudden and dispatch.
    Arthur. Are you sick, Hubert? you look pale to-day.
In sooth, I would you were a little sick,
That I might sit all night and watch with you:

I warrant I love you more than you do me.

    Hubert [*aside*]. His words do take possession of my
      bosom.

Read here, young Arthur. . . .   [*Showing a paper.*]

Can you not read it? Is it not fair writ?

    Arthur. Too fairly, Hubert, for so foul effect.

Must you with hot irons burn out both mine eyes?

    Hubert. Young boy, I must.

    Arthur.   And will you?

    Hubert.   And I will.

    Arthur. Have you the heart? When your head did but ache,

I knit my handkerchief about your brows—

The best I had, a princess wrought it me—

And I did never ask it you again;

And with my hand at midnight held your head,

And like the watchful minutes to the hour,

Still and anon cheer'd up the heavy time,

Saying, "What lack you?" and "Where lies your grief?"

Or "What good love may I perform for you?"

Many a poor man's son would have lain still,

And ne'er have spoke a loving word to you;

But you at your sick service had a prince.

Nay, you may think my love was crafty love,

And call it cunning. Do, an if you will.

If heaven be pleased that you must use me ill,

Why then you must. Will you put out mine eyes?

These eyes that never did nor never shall

So much as frown on you.

    Hubert.   I have sworn to do it;

And with hot irons must I burn them out.

    Arthur. Ah, none but in this iron age would do it!

The iron of itself, though heat red-hot,
Approaching near these eyes, would drink my tears
And quench its fiery indignation
Even in the matter of mine innocence;
Nay, after that, consume away in rust,
But for containing fire to harm mine eyes.
Are you more stubborn-hard than hammered iron?
An if an angel should have come to me
And told me Hubert should put out mine eyes,
I would not have believed him,—no tongue but Hubert's.

   Hubert. Come forth.   [*Stamps.*]

      [*Re-enter Attendants, with a cord, irons, etc.*]

Do as I bid you do.

   Arthur. O, save me, Hubert, save me! my eyes are out
Even with the fierce looks of these awful men.

   Hubert. Give me the iron, I say, and bind him here.

   Arthur. Alas, what need you be so boisterous-rough?
I will not struggle, I will stand stone-still.
For heaven sake, Hubert, let me not be bound!
Nay, hear me, Hubert, drive these men away,
And I will sit as quiet as a lamb;
I will not stir, nor wince, nor speak a word,
Nor look upon the iron angrily.
Thrust but these men away, and I'll forgive you,
Whatever torment you do put me to.

   Hubert. Go, stand within; leave me alone with him,

   Attendant. I am best pleased to be from such a deed.

                        [*Exeunt Attendants.*]

   Arthur. Alas, I then have chid away my friend!
He hath a stern look, but a gentle heart;

Let him come back, that his compassion may
Give life to yours.

    Hubert.   Come, boy, prepare yourself.

    Arthur. Is there no remedy?

    Hubert.   None, but to lose your eyes.

    Arthur. O heaven, that there were but a mote in yours,
A grain, a dust, a gnat, a wandering hair,
Any annoyance in that precious sense!
Then feeling what small things are harmful there,
Your vile intent must needs seem horrible.

    Hubert. Is this your promise? Go to, hold your tongue.

    Arthur. Hubert, the utterance of a brace of tongues
Must needs want pleading for a pair of eyes;
Let me not hold my tongue, let me not, Hubert;
Or, Hubert, if you will, cut out my tongue,
So I may keep mine eyes. O spare mine eyes,
Though to no use but still to look on you!
Lo, by my troth, the instrument is cold,
And would not harm me.

    Hubert.   I can heat it, boy.

    Arthur. No, in good sooth; the fire is dead with grief,
Being create for comfort, to be used
In undeserved extremes. See else yourself;
There is no malice in this burning coal;
The breath of heaven has blown its spirit out,
And strewed repentant ashes on its head.

    Hubert, But with my breath I can revive it, boy.

    Arthur. An if you do, you will but make it blush
And glow with shame of your proceedings, Hubert; ...
All things that you should use to do me wrong

Deny their office; only you do lack
That mercy which fierce fire and iron extend. . . .

 Hubert. Well, see to live; I will not touch thine eyes. . . .

 Arthur. O heaven! I thank you, Hubert.

 Hubert. Silence! No more. Go closely in with me;
Much danger do I undergo for thee.   [*Exeunt.*]

   Notes:

arras	=	curtains hung against a wall.
chide	=	to blame, scold.
dispatch	=	to act quickly.
mote	=	a particle of dust.
wantonness	=	affectation or sport.
warrant	=	something that gives authority.
only for wantonness	=	out of mere sportiveness.
by my Christendom	=	by my baptism or Christianity.
be sudden and dispatch	=	be quick in carrying out his orders.
fair writ	=	well written.
at your sick service	=	at your service during sickness.
in undeserved extremes	=	in acts of great cruelty.
an if	=	if.

 Shakespeare often uses shortened forms of participles—for example *heat, writ, create.* These are not to be imitated.

EXERCISES

1. Give briefly Arthur's reasons why his eyes should not be put out.
2. Answer the following questions:
  (*a*) What did Hubert order his attendants to do?
  (*b*) Where were they to hide till the signal was given for their entry?
  (*c*) Did Hubert like the work entrusted to him by the king?
  (*d*) How do you know he did not like it?
  (*e*) How had Arthur treated Hubert in the past?
  (*f*) What did he say when the attendants entered the room?
  (*g*) Did Arthur keep to his promise of not speaking a word? Why?

HUBERT AND ARTHUR.
(*From the picture by William F. Yeames, R.A.*)

    (*h*) What happened to the fire brought in for heating the iron rods?

    (*i*) What did Hubert finally say to Arthur?

    (*j*) Did he intend telling the king that he had not burnt out Arthur's eyes? Why?

3. Select twelve lines in different parts of the extract, and find out how many feet each line has, and where the strong beat comes in each foot. Are all the lines alike in this respect? Which pairs of lines end with rhymes?

LESSON 34

PLANT REPRODUCTION

PLANTS reproduce others of their kind naturally in many different ways, such as by seeds, tubers, rhizomes, offshoots, suckers, runners, and leaves. The most common way is, of course, by seeds.

Those plants which grow, flower, seed, and die in one year are known as *annuals*; usually they produce seeds in large numbers. Others, such as the carrot and the beetroot, do not produce seed in their first year. These plants store up food in their tap roots, by means of which they are able to make new growth in their second year, and then put forth flowers and seeds. Such plants are known as *biennials*, and they mostly grow in temperate climates.

A very large group of plants which live for many years are known as *perennials*. This group includes trees, shrubs, and herbs of various kinds. Sometimes it takes a considerable number of years for them to produce seeds. Occasionally they only do so when they have reached maturity, and then they die.

Coconut seed sprouting.

Certain kinds of palms, such as the Talipot of Sri Lanka, do this, as also does the Jamaica "mountain pride." There is probably a specimen of each of these in the Botanic Gardens in your country. If so, you should take note of it when flowers and seeds are being formed.

The agaves, which you should know well, are also a common example of this interesting habit. One kind of agave, cultivated on a large scale in the Bahamas, yields sisal hemp. In other islands you probably know plants like this by the name "langue bœuf" (*henequén* in Belize). Some bamboos also flower, seed, and die in a manner similar to that described.

In other lessons you have read of the means with which Nature has provided many plants for the dispersal of their seeds, and also for furnishing the young plants with a reserve of food until their roots are able to absorb food from the soil.

Arrowroot.

Some plants produce no seeds, or only very few, and such plants have therefore been supplied with other means by which they may increase. Common West Indian plants of this type are, yams, bananas, bougainvilleas, and sweet potatoes. You can probably add others to this list.

Tubers are one means by which plants multiply themselves. These are of two kinds—stem tubers and root tubers. The sweet potato is a root tuber, and the yam is a stem tuber. If a yam is cut into sections, new plants will grow from them, provided a piece of the outer skin remains attached.

Most tubers are produced below the ground, but some plants form them on the climbing stems. An instance of this may be found in the Lisbon yam, or the "cut-and-throw-away" yam. These produce aerial tubers at the bases of the leafstalks. They are often miscalled seeds in the West Indies.

A rhizome is a thick underground stem. Well-known examples are arrowroot, ginger, turmeric and "tousles mois." If broken up, these underground stems will form new plants, and we make much use of this method to propagate such plants. In some cases, of course, plants which have rhizomes also produce seeds, but the quicker and better method of increasing them is by pieces of their underground stems.

Bananas are propagated by suckers.

Many bulbous plants are propagated by off-shoots. On the mother plant below the ground, such plants form buds, each of which will develop into another plant the exact counterpart of its parent. We make use of this method regularly for growing crops of chives and shallots. The mother plant is taken up and used by man, and the off-shoots are planted again.

The banana is reproduced by suckers which arise in a somewhat similar manner. In Egypt the date-palm is usually grown from suckers, not, of course, because the plant does not produce seeds, but because in this case the seeds do not always form a tree producing fruits like those of the tree from which they were taken.

Some plants have long running stems which creep along the ground and at intervals send roots down into the soil and a new plant up into the air. These new plants are capable of existing apart from the parent, that is, each little plant will live by itself if the runner is broken. The savannah grass, so common on our pastures, spreads by this means, and so do the violet and the strawberry in temperate countries.

Base of Banana Plant, with Sucker.

In other cases plants are reproduced from their leaves, which when broken off, or when they fall naturally to the ground, are able to form roots and shoots to develop into new plants. The "leaf of life" is well known to you for this peculiarity. It will grow under very dry conditions, even if pinned to the wall of a room. The leaves of some fleshy begonias which grow in moist shady places will also produce new plants. Some ferns, too, form little plants on their fronds.

You have now learned how many different ways there are by which plants are reproduced naturally. There are other ways, however, which man has discovered, such as by cuttings, layering, budding, and grafting.

No doubt you will wonder why it is necessary to employ methods such as these when Nature has provided so many means of her own. Unfortunately the seeds of certain plants do not grow up to be plants exactly like the one from which they were taken, and there is often no natural means by which they can be propagated. In such cases one of these artificial methods is utilized.

If you are planting fruit trees it is very important to know beforehand exactly what kind of fruit they will bear,

Savannah Grass—Running Stem and Roots.

and to be sure of this we must bud, graft, layer, or put in cuttings instead of trying to grow the plants from seed. How this is done you will learn in another place, and the boys will probably put these methods into practice in their work in the school garden.

EXERCISES

1. Study the following:

Latin.	English.
annus	a year
bi	twice
per	through

    Why, therefore, are certain plants called "annuals," "biennials," or "perennials"?
2. Explain the difference between "natural" and "artificial." Give illustrations from methods of plant reproduction.
3. Make a drawing of a banana plant with its sucker.

4. Complete the following table:

Method of Propagation.	Examples of Plants usually Produced by this Means.
seeds	....
tubers	....
rhizomes	....
off-shoots.	....
suckers.	....
runners.	....
leaves	....
budding	....
grafting	....
layering	....
cuttings	....

5. Count the seeds on a good cob of corn. Suppose a plant bears three cobs like this one, and from each seed a similar plant is produced, how many corn plants would one plant produce in five years if all the seeds were sown each year?

6. The following are often called roots—yams, ginger, arrow-root, sweet potatoes, turmeric. What are they really?

7. Fill in the blanks:
   (a) When plants are grown from ——, they are often very different from the —— plant which produced the ——.
   (b) Some —— do not produce ——, and therefore they must be —— in other ways.
   (c) A piece of a plant which, when cut —— and —— into the soil, starts to grow is known as a ——.
   (d) Many tubers are used as food; some are called stem ——, and others root ——. ——belong to the first class, and —— to the latter.
   (e) The most common way of —— plants is by ——. This is a —— way, whereas budding and —— are —— means.

LESSON 35

THE ISLAND WHICH BECAME
A BATTLESHIP
—H.M.S. *DIAMOND ROCK*

BETWEEN St. Lucia and Martinique there stands an isolated rock, which rises sheer out of the water off the south coast of the latter island. No member of the British Navy can gaze upon it without a feeling of pride, for it is the historic Diamond Rock. During the war with France in 1803 it was garrisoned by the crew of a British cruiser, who hauled their guns to its summit by means of ropes, and defied their adversaries.

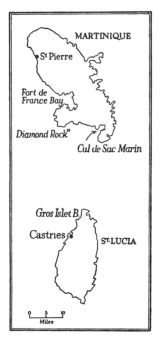

Commodore Sir Samuel Hood had established a blockade of Fort de France, then Fort Royal, from which De Grasse had sailed twenty years earlier to meet defeat at the Battle of the Saints. Hood found that the French ships were eluding him by slipping away between the Diamond Rock and the Point du Diamant, and therefore laid his seventy-four, the *Centaur*, close alongside the rock, where she was kept in position by anchors laid out fore and aft and lines fastened to the shore by means of grapnels. A life-line was then shot to the top of the rock, and by it a heavier rope was drawn up, and finally a great cable, which served as a stay.

A secure purchase was next fastened to the rock, travellers were cleverly arranged to pass along the stay, the guns were lashed to these travellers, and then, with many a "Heave-ho" and "All together," the heavy masses of metal were slowly but successfully hoisted up to their airy embrasures. By the end of the third day three long twenty-fours and two eighteens were at the summit, and Fort Diamond was gunned, garrisoned, and provisioned, and ready for operations offensive and defensive.

An eye-witness of this wonderful feat describes "how along a dire, and I had almost said a perpendicular acclivity, the sailors are hanging in clusters, hauling up a four-and-twenty pounder by hawsers. They appear like mice hauling a little sausage; scarcely can we hear the Governor on the top, directing them with his trumpet, the *Centaur* lying close under it, like a coconut shell."

There is a tradition that Diamond Rock was formally put in commission as a sloop of war, and rated as such upon the books of the navy, during the eighteen months that Capt. J. W. Maurice with 120 men and boys remained on it.

The sailors enjoyed their life there so much that it was with difficulty they could be persuaded to return to their ship periodically. The rock proved healthy despite the presence of the fer-de-lance, and life passed pleasantly. Occasionally the parent ship would creep into Fort Royal Bay to cut out an enemy vessel, and there were great

DIAMOND ROCK.

rejoicings on the rock when she returned one day with the *Curieux* as a prize under her wing.

The garrison remained on the rock harassing the enemy on every possible opportunity until January 2, 1805, when, through want of ammunition and water, they were compelled to surrender to a French squadron of two seventy-fours, a 36-gun frigate, a 16-gun corvette, and eleven gunboats each mounting three cannon, and a force of from three to four hundred troops. They did not capitulate, however, until they had inflicted severe loss on the enemy, wounding seventy men and destroying three gunboats, while they themselves lost only two men killed and one wounded. Honourable terms were agreed to, and the gallant Maurice and his men marched out of the Queen's Battery on the rock with drums beating and colours flying, and having laid down their arms, embarked on a French vessel and were sent to Barbados, where Nelson had just arrived, in his pursuit of Villeneuve, of which we read in Book III.

.   .   .   .

The following extract from the story *Diamond Rock*, which all boys would love to read, gives an account of an incident during the occupation of the rock:

They were beginning to find the island rather dull, when, on a bright morning in March, the look-out at the peak reported the approach of a number of vessels sailing in company.

"A French convoy, ten chances to one!" exclaimed Captain Maurice. "Just what we've been waiting for. Now then, let us get ready to give them a warm reception."

It proved to be a squadron of French and Spanish ships returning in triumph to Martinique after doing damage at Dominica and St. Kitts, and securing considerable plunder. The spectacle presented was certainly an imposing one, as fifteen sail of the line (eight being Spanish and seven French), with a whole cloud of frigates, schooners, and smaller craft in attendance, bore down in orderly array for Cul de Sac Marin, knowing nothing of the wasps' nest that had been established off its entrance.

Intense was the excitement, but perfect the discipline, at the British stronghold. There would be work for all this morning, the manifest purpose of the squadron being to pass to both right and left of the little island that looked so innocent of harm. On they came before a steady breeze, until they were well within range of the Queen's and Gryphon Batteries. Then the Union Jack suddenly climbed to the top of the signal mast, and as its folds flung out upon the breeze, the twenty-four pounders spoke together, and their iron missiles, with admirable aim, went crashing into the sides of the two leading ships.

The amazement and alarm of those on board the fleet would be difficult to picture. They could not have been more surprised had their own admiral turned his guns upon them. No hint had they received of their foes having found a foothold so close to one of their own possessions. Yet there was the British flag flaunting itself in their faces, and that was British thunder and British iron beyond a doubt.

What did it mean? How great was the strength of the forces upon the island? Did the rock bristle with cannon and bayonets, like a gigantic hedgehog; or were there only a gun or two, and a handful of daring men who would soon be made to pay dearly for their temerity? In lively perturbation the French and Spanish admirals and their captains scanned Diamond Rock with their telescopes. But peer as eagerly as they might, nothing could they make out save a glint of white as a sailor moved through the thick foliage, or the flash of the cannon that meantime kept up a steady, well-directed fire.

Dick and Tenderly,[*] with ten good men, were at the summit training the long eighteen-pounders downward until they pointed straight at their mark, and then sending shot after shot through the sails or into the decks of the approaching vessels.

"My eye," Dick shouted, "but this is glorious! What would Bony[†] think if he could only see us knocking the splinters out of his fine ships in this style?—Well done, Tom!" turning to big Tom Taffrail, the gunner, who had just sent a shot smash into the bulwarks of a Spanish ship of the line. "That was a beauty! What a bewildered lot of blocks they must be, to be sure!"

The fire from the rock was terribly destructive. The wind was such that the vessels could not bear away. Their only chance was to keep straight on until they could pass beyond range; and as luck would have it, the breeze fell before they could all accomplish this, leaving a group of them right under the batteries.

In the whole history of the British navy there probably never was such an extraordinary target practice; for

[*] Two characters in the story.
[†] Napoleon Bonaparte.

THE TWENTY-FOUR POUNDERS SPOKE TOGETHER.

(*See page 229.*)

although the ships replied to the best of their ability, they might just as well have saved their ammunition. Their tormentors were so high above them that only mortars could reach them, and the fleet had no mortars on board. So they were fain to content themselves with fierce and futile pounding at the foot of the cliffs, while Captain Maurice and his merry men, safely ensconced above the line of fire, pegged away without the distraction of having to dodge an iron hail.

Presently the wind rose, the white sails of the ships and schooners bellied out before it, they began one by one to glide out of range, and within two hours from the time it began the fight was over. With sails torn, rigging damaged, bulwarks splintered, decks pierced, and many men killed and wounded, the allied squadron sailed into Cul de Sac Marin, having on board the maddest lot of men that ever were afloat.

    .   .   .   .

The actual letters which passed between Captain Maurice and Lord Nelson after the surrender of the rock are given below:

I

BARBADOES,[*]
6th June, 1805.

MY LORD,

     It is with the greatest sorrow I have to inform you of the loss of the Diamond Rock under my command, which was obliged to surrender on the 2nd instant, after

_____

[*] Note old spelling of Barbados.

three days' attack from a squadron of two sail of the line, one frigate, one brig, a schooner, eleven gunboats, and, from the nearest calculation, 1,500 troops. The want of ammunition and water was the sole occasion of this unfortunate loss. Although I shall never cease to regret the accident, yet it is some consolation to think so many valuable lives are saved to His Majesty's service, having only two killed and one wounded. The enemy, from the nearest account I have been able to obtain, lost on shore thirty killed and forty wounded, independent of the ships and boats; they also lost three gunboats and two rowing-boats. Allow me to speak in the highest terms of the officers and men under my command, and I trust, when the court-martial shall have taken place, that their hardships, fatigue, and gallantry will merit your lordship's approbation, they having been nineteen nights under arms. I beg leave to enclose the articles of capitulation.

I have the honour to remain, etc.,

J. W. MAURICE

To the Right Hon. Viscount Nelson, etc., etc.

Articles of Capitulation

I. That the rock, with all its works, shall be delivered up entire.

II. That the garrison shall be allowed to march to the Queen's Battery with drums beating and colours flying, and there lay down their arms.

III. That all private property shall be secured to the officers and men.

IV. That the garrison shall be sent to Barbadoes, at the expense of the French nation; but not to serve till regularly exchanged.

V. That the garrison is capable of holding out a few days longer, and two hours are given for an answer, when hostilities will be recommenced.

J. W. MAURICE.

II

"VICTORY," AT SEA,
8th June, 1805.

SIR,

I have received your letter of the 6th instant, acquainting me with the surrender of the Diamond Rock under your command, on the 2nd of this month, to a squadron of the enemy's ships and gunboats therein mentioned, together with the terms of capitulation which accompanied your said letter. In answer to which, while I regret the loss of the Diamond, I have no doubt that every exertion has been used by your-self, and those under your command, for its defence, and that its surrender has been occasioned from the circumstances you represent. It is particularly gratifying that so few lives were lost in the contest, and I have very fully to express my approbation of the terms of capitulation, as well as with your conduct personally, and that of the officers and men under your command, which I have to request you will be pleased to communicate to them.

I am, Sir,
Your most obedient humble servant,
NELSON AND BRONTE.

Exercise

(Note to Teacher.—Allow five minutes for the test.)

In this test wherever a number appears there is one word, and only one word, missing. Write each word opposite to its proper number.

The war between England and (1) was now at its height, and (2) nation was straining every effort to crush the other. (3), too, had taken a hand in the (4), entering into alliance with France against (5), and thereby greatly increasing the (6) of the British navy, which had henceforth to be (7) over a wider space, and its strength divided.

Counting upon this, Napoleon, who had hitherto attempted little in the line of (8) operations, dispatched a powerful fleet to the West Indies, with the object of harassing the (9) possessions there, even though (10) conquest might not be accomplished. Being joined by a number of Spanish (11), the squadron managed to elude the British (12), and at Dominica and St. Kitts did a good deal of (13), besides securing considerable plunder, with (14) it was returning in (15) to Martinique when (16) by the lookout on Diamond Rock.

MOTHER AND SON. (*Chardin*.)

LESSON 36

PICTURE LESSONS—VII

MOTHER AND SON

CHARDIN, the French artist who painted this picture in 1735, had little imagination, but he had a fine sense of form and colour. He was marvellously skilful in painting, and made delightful pictures out of such small matters as a few apples on a cloth, or an old copper bucket under a stool; his landscapes and groups of people are exquisite.

The "Mother and Son" is a beautiful picture in drawing, light and shade, and colour. But we are concerned rather with the way in which the artist composed it than with these excellent qualities.

In the first place, as there are two persons equally important, the mother and the son, the artist brings them towards the centre of his canvas. The mother's white cap and apron draw the attention first towards her, but in a moment we leave her to look at the son; for the artist connects the two in many ways by lines that run round about and across both figures, as you may see by the sketch on page 238. For instance, the curve at the bottom of the boy's full coat swings round into the lower rim of the hat, and so on through the mother's arm and round to her head. Thence by a line in the wainscoting of the door it comes to the boy's head, and so completes its ellipse or oval.

The mother's figure is so much larger than the boy's that the artist takes special care to "bring him out" to arrest attention to him. This is done by drawing many strong, upright lines about him. First there is the strong blue of the open doorway; then there are the lines of the door and the panelling, and on the floor below are some little bright things—red and white shuttlecock, red and white battledore, and red and white cards—cheerful spots to catch the eye and draw it towards the boy. You will notice, too, that the packet which sticks out of the work-basket on the floor points towards the hat, and so on to the boy; for none of these slight things are put in without a purpose, which is to make the picture complete in composition.

Then there is *contrast*. See how well the black hat shows against the white apron, and how there are everywhere curved lines against straight.

LESSON 37

THE SEA-KING'S BURIAL

Introduction.—The Vikings were those old warriors of the sea whose home was in the part of Europe called Scandinavia. We seem to feel something of their fierce spirit as we read this fine poem. The burial of a Viking chief was a soul-stirring event; his body was placed in a boat which, with full sail set and a fire kindled, was sent drifting out to sea. The chieftain was supposed to enter Valhalla, the home of the gods, as the fire slowly consumed the vessel and the body of the dead.

In this poem the last journey of King Balder was even more tragic, for the king was not dead when he set sail on his funeral voyage for Valhalla, but he went forth voluntarily to his fate. He is named after one of the gods in the old myths and legends of Norway, and despite the fact that the Vikings were pagans, we are forced to admire their indomitable spirit, and the noble bravery of their imaginary gods of which we read in their stories.

This poem was written by Charles Mackay, a well-known poet and journalist, who was born in 1814 and died in 1889.

> "MY strength is failing fast,"
>   Said the sea-king to his men.
> "I shall never sail the seas
>   Like a conqueror again;
> But while yet a drop remains
> Of the life-blood in my veins,
> Raise, oh, raise me from my bed,
> Put the crown upon my head,
> Put my good sword in my hand,
> And so lead me to the strand
>   Where my ship at anchor rides
>   Steadily;
> If I cannot end my life
> In the crimsoned battle-strife,
>   Let me die as I have lived,
>   On the sea."

They have raised King Balder up,
    Put the crown upon his head;
They have sheathed his limbs in mail
    And the purple o'er him spread;
And, amid the greeting rude
Of a gathering multitude,
Borne him slowly to the shore,
All the energy of yore
From his dim eyes flashing forth,
Old sea-lion of the North,
    As he looked upon his ship
            Riding free,
And on his forehead pale
Felt the cold, refreshing gale,
    And heard the welcome sound
            Of the sea.

They have borne him to the ship
    With a slow and solemn tread;
They have placed him on the deck
    With his crown upon his head,
Where he sat as on a throne;
And have left him there alone,
With his anchor ready weighed,
And his snowy sails displayed
To the favouring wind, once more
Blowing freshly from the shore;
    And have bidden him farewell
            Tenderly,
Saying: "King of mighty men,
We shall meet thee yet again
    In Valhalla, with the monarchs
            Of the sea."

Underneath him, in the hold,
    They have placed the lighted brand;

A GREAT VIKING. (*Hoekkuk.*)

And the fire was burning slow
  As the vessel from the land,
Like a stag-hound from the slips,
Darted forth from out the ships.
There was music in her sail
As it swelled before the gale,
And a dashing at her prow
As it cleft the waves below,
  And the good ship sped along,
    Scudding free;
As on many a battle morn
In her time she had been borne
  To struggle and to conquer
    On the sea.

And the king, with sudden strength
  Started up and paced the deck,
With his good sword for his staff,
  And his robe around his neck.
Once alone, he raised his hand
To the people on the land;
And with shout and joyous cry
Once again they made reply,
Till the loud, exulting cheer
Sounded faintly in his ear;
  For the gale was o'er him blowing
    Fresh and free;
And ere yet an hour had passed
He was driven before the blast,
  And a storm was in his path
    On the sea.

"So blow, ye tempests, blow,
  And my spirit shall not quail;
I have fought with many a foe,
  I have weathered many a gale;

And in this hour of death,
Ere I yield my fleeting breath,
Ere the fire now burning slow
Shall come rushing down below.
And this worn and wasted frame
Be devoted to the flame,
    I will raise my voice in triumph,
           Singing free;
To the great All-Father's home
I am driving through the foam,
    I am sailing to Valhalla
          O'er the sea.

"So blow, ye stormy winds,
    And ye flames, ascend on high;
In easy, idle bed
    Let the slave and coward die!
But give me the driving keel,
Clang of shields and flashing steel,
Or my foot on foreign ground,
With my enemies around!
Happy, happy, thus I'd yield,
On the deck or in the field,
    My last breath shouting, On
          To victory.
But since this has been denied,
They shall say that I have died
    Without flinching, like a monarch
          Of the sea."

And Balder spoke no more,
    And no sound escaped his lip;
And he looked, yet scarcely saw
    The destruction of his ship,
Nor the fleet sparks mounting high.
Nor the glare upon the sky;

Scarcely heard the billows dash,
Nor the burning timber crash;
Scarcely felt the scorching heat
That was gathering at his feet,
    Nor the fierce flames mounting o'er him
                Greedily.
But the life was in him yet,
And the courage to forget
    All his pain in his triumph
                On the sea.

Once alone, a cry arose,
    Half of anguish, half of pride,
As he sprang upon his feet,
    With the flames on every side.
"I am coming!" said the king,
"Where the swords and bucklers ring,
Where the warrior lives again,
Where the souls of mighty men
And the weary find repose,
And the red wine ever flows.
    I am coming, great All-Father,
                Unto Thee!
Unto Odin, unto Thor,
And the strong, true hearts of yore:
    I am coming to Valhalla
                O'er the sea."

CHARLES MACKAY.

EXERCISES

1. Find Scandinavia on the map of Europe. What countries now
   form Scandinavia?
2. The Vikings lived as farmers in harvest and seed-time, but
   in the times between fared forth as sea-robbers, raiders,
   and settlers. There is little doubt they reached the mainland
   of America 500 years before Columbus. Their sea-route

by way of Iceland was shorter than that of the Genoese seaman. Trace it on a map, or, better still, on a globe. In what part did they land?

3. "Thor "was their God of Thunder; "Odin" (or Woden) the God of War. Two of the days of the week are named after them. Which are they?

4. Tell the story in two ways:
   (i.) as a spectator;
   (ii.) in the words of Balder himself.

LESSON 38

SUGAR MANUFACTURE

WE have already read of the cultivation of sugar-cane and in this lesson we shall see what happens to the canes after they leave the field. The sugar-growing parts of Guyana are very flat, and the country is intersected by a network of water-ways for drainage purposes. Thus the canes can easily be conveyed to the factory in large iron punts or scows on those streams, or punt-trenches as they are called. In the islands railways are used on the large estates, whilst mules, horses, oxen, or donkeys provide the means of transport for the small cane-farmers. Animal traction is also used from the fields to the loading stations even on large estates.

Sugar-cane, as you know, contains a large quantity (about nine-tenths of its weight) of a sweet, sticky juice, which owes its sweet taste to its sugar. This juice consists of more than five times as much water as sugar, and it also contains impurities, such as salts, acids, gums, and albumen. The objects of the factory, therefore, are to extract the juice from the cane, to remove the acids and other impurities, to get rid of the surplus water, and to obtain sugar in the form of crystals from the remaining liquid. Let us now follow the cane through the factory and see how these things are done.

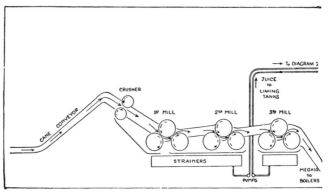

DIAGRAM SHOWING THE ARRANGEMENT OF A MODERN

On reaching the factory the canes are weighed, lifted out of their wagons by machinery, and placed on a travelling band or "carrier," which conveys them to the mouth of the crushing machine, known as a "three-roller" mill, driven by steam or electric power. This machine consists of two ponderous iron rollers placed side by side, with a space between them and another above nearly touching them. The lower rollers revolve in the same direction and the upper one in the opposite direction. The diagram on this page will make this clear to you. It also shows you that, in order to extract as much juice as possible, the cane is passed through several of these three-roller mills, the space between the rollers becoming slightly smaller for each successive crushing. The number of mills thus arranged varies from one to six, but in an efficient factory the number is usually four.

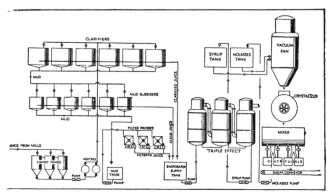

SUGAR MILL. (*From a drawing by Mr. W. Scott, B.Sc.*)

Before entering the first mill the cane is cracked and broken by passing through two other rollers, known as "crushers," which, with three mills as shown, form an "eleven-roller" mill. Besides the crusher, modern factories use other forms of preparation for cane, such as rotating knives and shredders.

The juice is caught in a trough below the mills, and flows to a vessel where it is roughly strained from the finely divided cane fibre which falls down with it, and is then pumped up to the "liming tanks." The almost dry fibre, called "megass" or "bagasse," which remains after the crushing, goes straight to the boiler-house, where it is used as fuel to heat the boilers which provide the steam-power for the whole factory.

Among other things which the greenish-coloured juice contains are certain organisms which would cause it to ferment if left exposed to the air for even half an hour. It would then be acid and quite unfit for use. The next process, therefore, is to remove these impurities. This is done in the liming-tanks, where the juice is measured and mixed with a certain quantity of lime, which destroys the acidity of the juice.

From the liming-tanks the juice is passed through juice-heaters, and heated to the boiling-point of water or slightly over. It then proceeds through a pipe to large vats called "clarifiers," where it is allowed to settle for an hour or more. Suspended matter, such as fibre, wax, colouring matter, and the dirt which had adhered to the canes, settles with the albumen to the bottom, and a scum rises to the surface. After the juice has settled, the clear juice between the *top* and *bottom* layers of mud is drawn off and sent (usually after screening through a fine gauze) to the evaporator.

You will be able to follow these processes easily on the diagram on pages 246 and 247. There you will note the arrangement provided for passing the mud and scum into other vats, from which, after settling again, more clear juice is obtained. From these "mud sub-sliders," as they are called, the mud goes to powerful filter presses, which extract from it practically all the juice remaining.

Having thus purified the cane juice, the next step is to evaporate the water as quickly as possible to enable the sugar to crystallize. The liquor is therefore drawn through pipes into the "multiple effect" an apparatus consisting of a series of closed vessels, in which the liquor is boiled to

A MODERN SUGAR-MILL.

concentrate or thicken it. In the diagram a "triple effect" (three vessels) is shown; many factories use a "quadruple effect" (four vessels). The syrup, as the thick juice is now called, is then transferred to the vacuum pan.

This is a closed vessel made so that the air can be pumped out of it, with the result that the water boils or changes into vapour at a much lower temperature than it does in an open vessel. The boiling is continued until small grains or crystals of sugar can be seen through a little glass window in the pan. Samples of the liquor are also taken from the pan by a "proof-stick" to test the progress of crystallization.

After the crystals appear the mixture of sugar crystals and the mother liquor is called "massecuite." When this massecuite becomes of the correct thickness, the vacuum pan is "struck" or tapped at the bottom, the contents being transferred to the centrifugals. These are large drums with perforated or meshed sides somewhat like wire baskets, which are whirled round some 1200 times to the minute. The result of this rapid rotation is that the molasses is driven out of the drums through the meshes of the wire by centrifugal force, leaving the sugar behind in the form of greyish-yellow crystals.

This sugar is packed in jute bags, each containing a certain weight, and is then ready for shipment to all parts of the world. The molasses is again boiled and made into lower grades of sugar, called second and third sugars, or is used to make rum or cattle food.

All the large estates and modern sugar factories adopt the process which has been described, and which is known as the Vacuum Pan process. There are still, however, a number of small estates where a much older method, the Muscovado process, is yet practised. The canes are crushed

Evaporator.

by less elaborate machinery, and the juice is treated with lime and cleansed much in the same way as in the newer process.

The later stages differ, however, for the clarified juice then flows down to the "copper wall," a series of three or more large open copper tanks over fires or furnaces, called "tayches," in which the evaporation of the liquor takes place. The juice is ladled by dippers from the first tayche to the second, and then on to the third. When it has become thick enough it is placed in large square boxes called coolers, where it remains for a week or two. During this time the sugar forms into solid grains, and when quite cool it is dug out and put into hogsheads with holes at the bottom, which are kept open by pieces of green plantain stalks For about four weeks the hogsheads remain in a room adjoining the boiling-house, while the molasses drains through the holes into large cisterns.

After this period the casks are then headed up, and their contents, known as Muscovado sugar, are ready for shipment.

The molasses obtained by this method is of a much higher quality than that which is produced by the vacuum process. The flavour is better, and it finds a ready market in Canada and Newfoundland, especially in the latter place, where the hardy fishermen who catch and send us our "salt-fish" use it freely. Barbados exports much more of this commodity than any other West Indian country.

EXERCISES

1. The word "tapped" may mean either "knocked" or "opened by a tap." Which meaning has it in this lesson?
2. State exactly what is the use of each of the following: crushers, eleven-roller mill, carrier, clarifiers, lime, filters, triple effect, vacuum pan, centrifugals, tayches, hogsheads, coolers, and the copper wall.
3. What are the main differences between the Vacuum Pan process and the Muscovado process?
4. What is made from molasses? Where is molasses sold in its raw state?
5. What are the four chief steps in the manufacture of sugar?
6. Fill in the blanks in the following passages:
    (a) The Vacuum —— process of —— manufacture, which can be seen in British ——, J——, T——, A——, St. L——, and to a lesser extent in B——, is altogether more elaborate than the —— process.
    (b) The megass or —— is taken direct to the ——, where it is used as fuel.
    (c) An old writer, describing the donkeys bringing the canes to the mill, compared them to bees, the one fetching home ——, the other ——.
    (d) J—— and D—— have long been noted for their ——. This is made from molasses and the skimmings of the hot cane ——. Its well-known brown —— is given to it by —— a little burnt sugar.

(e) A planter in the old days has been known to keep ——
     in a bottle for two or —— years, at the end of which
     —— it was found to be perfectly good. Its flavour
     was —— than that of —— obtained by the newer
     process.

7. During the year 1926 the exports of sugar-cane products
    from the West Indies were as shown in this table:

	Sugar (tons).	Molasses (gals.).	Rum (gals.).
Antigua	11,466	393,178	–
Barbados	47,450	7,869,275	13,292
British Guiana	84,693	2,017,862	789,643
Jamaica	48,154	1,650	693,435
Montserrat.	28	3,559	–
St. Lucia.	5,214	156,424	37
St. Kitts and Nevis . .	15,710	467,762	–
St. Vincent	375	337,099	–
Trinidad.	65,679	1,427,274	71,213

Study these figures, and then arrange the colonies in their
order of importance in the sugar trade. In which colonies
is the molasses further treated to obtain rum etc.? In which
colonies is little rum made?

LESSON 39

INSECT PESTS—II

(a) INSECTS WHICH ATTACK MAN

Mosquitoes.—All of us who live in the West Indies
are familiar with mosquitoes, as they cause us much
annoyance in their endeavours to feed upon our blood.
These small insects are dangerous pests, as it has been
proved during recent years that they are carriers of such

diseases as malaria, filaria, and yellow fever—in fact, so far as is known they are the only means by which these diseases can be transmitted from one human being to another. The three common kinds in the West Indies are

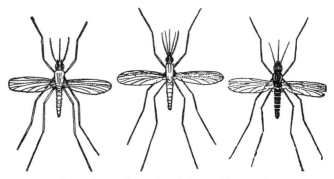

Mosquitoes—Culex, Anopheles, and Stegomyia.

(1) *culex,* which carries the filarial parasite, producing fever and ague often resulting in deformations of the limbs known as Barbados leg or elephantiasis; (2) *anopheles,* the carrier of malaria; (3) *stegomyia,* which transmits yellow fever.

Larva of Mosquito, showing breathing-tube projecting upwards.

As we have learnt in previous lessons, mosquitoes breed in stagnant or slowly running water, on the surface of which they lay their eggs. The three first stages of their life, egg, larva, and pupa, are spent in water. The larvæ and pupæ breathe by means of air-tubes, and it is necessary for them to come to the surface in order to do so. You can see the breathing organ in the drawing on this page, where it is shown as a projection at right angles to the body. If oil is poured on the surface of water containing larvæ and pupæ, they are unable to obtain air by these tubes, and are thus destroyed.

Only the female mosquitoes are capable of piercing the skin and sucking the blood of animals. The mouth parts of the male are adapted for sucking the juices of flowers.

In order to get rid of mosquitoes, all stagnant water and all receptacles or crevices which will hold water should be removed. The attacks of the adult mosquito can be prevented by the use of nets over the beds, or by screening the doors and windows of dwellings.

Flea, adult (much enlarged).

Fleas are trouble-some little insects which are found all over the world on most warmblooded animals. They cause much annoyance to human beings by hiding in clothing and bedding, from whence they emerge at night to pierce the skin and suck the blood of their victim.

Certain species of fleas play an important part in the transmission of a very serious disease—bubonic plague. This disease attacks rats, and the germs are absorbed by the fleas which live upon those animals. When a plague-infested rat dies the fleas leave its body in search of other food, and if they bite human beings they inject plague germs into them, which often cause death in a few days.

There is one little flea called the *Jigger Flea* (or *Chigoe*), the female of which before laying her eggs burrows into the skin of human beings, usually between the toes, and

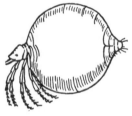

causes great itching and pain. This is due to the fact that as the eggs develop, the body of the female increases greatly in size until it becomes almost as large as a good-sized pea. The jigger should be removed from the

Jigger Flea (enlarged).

flesh as soon as its presence is discovered, care being taken not to burst the body in so doing.

The Bed Bug.—This disgusting and annoying insect is found in almost all countries, and is especially common in old houses or huts, from which it is hard to remove, as owing to its flat structure it can hide in the smallest

of crevices, such as cracks or joints in the framework of beds, floors, or walls, and in mattresses and pillows. Bed bugs have the power of living for long periods even without human blood for food, and old beds which have been stored away for some time have been found to be infested with them. These insects can be destroyed by kerosene, which should

Bed Bug (enlarged).

be applied liberally and frequently on all the joints and crevices of any bed where signs of them have been seen. Remember, however, that kerosene takes fire easily, so it is necessary to be very careful when it is used in a house.

Other Pests.—Among other insects which attack man are the various forms of *lice,* and those minute reddish mites, *bête rouge,*[*] which occur in grass and shrubs, and attack the ankles and wrists of persons exposed to them.

(*b*) PESTS OF DOMESTIC ANIMALS

Domestic animals in the tropics are attacked by insects and other pests to a greater extent than similar animals are in cooler climates. In the small islands of the West Indies, however, certain of these pests are less troublesome than in larger tropical countries. The *cattle ticks* are examples of such pests. Although common in our islands, they do not cause so much damage as in other parts of the world, where they are the source of great loss to cattle raisers and estate owners, because of the irritation to the cattle and the loss of blood taken as food by enormous numbers of these parasites.

Cattle Tick (enlarged).

The cattle tick is one of the mites, and not a true insect, as the adult has four pairs of legs. Each female produces great numbers of eggs—from 1,500 to 3,000—which it lays on the ground. The young larvæ cluster upon grass and low herbage, where they await the passing of cattle or other animals to which they may attach themselves. They are then known as grass-lice or grass-ticks. As soon as they find themselves on a suitable host they begin at once to suck its blood.

[*] Belize, *red bugs.*

Cattle ticks also attack horses, goats, and dogs, but not in sufficient numbers to be considered pests. They may, however, transmit diseases of such animals. Dogs are also attacked by the *dog tick,* whilst the *gold tick* is common on animals in Antigua.

Fowls in the West Indies are often attacked by the *fowl tick,* a flattish grey mite, which hides in crevices under boards and comes out to prey upon the birds at night.

Cats and dogs are subject to the attacks of *fleas,* which in the adult stage live among the hairs of the body, and obtain their food by sucking the blood of their host. They have a similar life history to that of the house flea. The eggs are dropped on the floor or the ground, where they hatch and where the grub-like maggots live and develop.

(c) HOUSEHOLD INSECTS AND PESTS OF STORED PRODUCTS

Cockroaches are very common throughout the tropics, where they live in houses and buildings of all sorts.

Australian Cockroach. Male, female, and immature insect (reduced).

They are very offensive and injurious, as they impart their disagreeable odour to eatables or utensils with which they may come into contact, and they cause serious injury by their attacks on book-bindings, clothing, foodstuffs, and other things.

The common cockroaches are from one and a half to two inches long, and their wings have a spread of nearly four inches. They frequently appear on moist, hot nights in the wet season; the young ones can be seen in numbers if one enters a kitchen or storeroom at night, carrying a light. Boracic acid scattered freely where there are cockroaches acts as a very efficient check to this pest. They devour it readily and soon die.

The *silver fish,* or fish moth, is familiar to most residents of the West Indies. These insects infest books, papers, and photographs, to which they seem to be attracted by the starch or paste such articles contain. Bookbinders in the tropics should use a special paste to prevent the binding being eaten by these pests. Moth balls or camphor balls are useful in keeping them out of drawers, presses, boxes, bookshelves, and similar places.

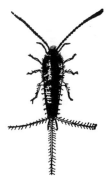

Silver Fish.

Ants are perhaps the most numerous of all household pests. There are several species, among which are the very minute *sugar ant,* which is pale reddish in colour and attacks sugar, jams, and similar substances; the so-called *red* or *stinging ant*; the *mad* or *crazy ant*, which is a slender, black insect with long legs; and the large, stout, dark-coloured ant, which lives in timbers and weakens them by its excavations.

The *termites* or so-called *white ants* or *wood ants* are not true ants. These insects are nearly always blind, and they hide from the light.

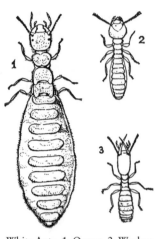

They build tunnels or covered galleries, through which they travel from place to place. They feed upon wood, and often render the timber in buildings entirely worthless by their depredations. Picture frames, chairs, tables, or other furniture which is not often moved is also frequently subject to their attacks, whilst they attack books and bore through the entire thickness from cover to cover.

White Ant—1. Queen. 2. Worker. 3. Soldier.

Among other pests are the *clothes moth,* whose caterpillars feed on articles of clothing such as woollens, furs, and feathers; the *drug-store beetle,* which attacks books,

cardboard boxes, picture frames, cereals, food-stuffs and seeds, as well as other articles of many different natures; the *cigarette beetle,* which has a wide range of food materials, similar to the

Cigarette Beetle, Larva and Adult.

drug-store beetle; *grain weevils,* which cause considerable injury to seeds, such as corn, peas, and beans; and the *ripe fruit flies,* which lay their eggs in and feed upon ripe fruits.

EXERCISES

1. What do you mean by an insect pest?
2. Study the drawings of the three mosquitoes. What differences do you notice? What other differences between the *culex* and the *anopheles* have you read of before in these Readers?
3. It is a common sight in the West Indies to find holes bored right through the covers and pages of a book. What has done this? How can you prevent it?
4. Make a list of all the pests named in this lesson, and show by the side of each what it preys upon.
5. What pests do you know which attack man through his bare feet?
6. Fill in as many examples as you can in this table of Animal Enemies of Man (animals include insects).

Animal.	Disease caused.	Place where the young ones live, or their breeding place.	Methods of removal or prevention.

7. Fill in the blanks:
   (*a*) We learn how to control insect pests of —— in our Nature Study lessons, but the methods of preventing pests of human —— are taught in our —— lessons.
   (*b*) Most —— like dirt and rubbish, in which they often lay their ——, and in which their —— develop.
   (*c*) It is important, therefore, to —— your body and —— regularly, and to keep your bed, house, —— and —— around your house, —— and free from collections of ——.
   (*d*) People stand the —— of a table or safe in —— containing water and —— to prevent —— attacking its contents.

(*e*) The mites which attack poultry are sometimes called —— in the West ——. They hide about the roosting —— during the day, but swarm out to feed at ——.

LESSON 40

"THE MERCHANT OF VENICE"
(*See Frontispiece*)

Introduction.—The story of Shakespeare's play, *The Merchant of Venice,* is briefly this. Antonio was a Christian merchant in the city of Venice. His dear friend Bassanio, who was about to marry a great heiress, Portia, wanted a loan of three thousand ducats to meet the expenses of the wedding. As Antonio had not the money to lend his friend, he asked Shylock, a Jewish money-lender, to let him have the sum, on the security of some ships laden with merchandise which he expected home soon. Now Shylock hated Antonio, because he was kind to people in trouble, and lent them money without taking interest. So, pretending to be very friendly, he offered to lend the required sum without interest, only insisting that Antonio should sign a bond—as a jest—that if he did not repay the money by a certain day he would forfeit a pound of flesh, to be cut from any part of his body. Antonio signed the bond and obtained the money for Bassanio. When Bassanio was about to be married to Portia, news came to him that Antonio's ships had been lost, and that his friend's bond to the Jew had been forfeited. Portia, on hearing this, decided to try to save her lover's friend at all costs. Having obtained from a legal acquaintance the robes of a lawyer, and also much advice as to how she should act, she went to Venice with her maid, Nerissa, and spoke in defence of Antonio. The following scene is part of the famous *Trial Scene* (Act IV. scene i.), in which Portia appears as a Doctor of Laws and saves Antonio from the clutches of the Jew. The Duke of Venice, Antonio, Bassanio, Shylock, and others are present.

SCENE—Venice: a Court of Justice.

[*Enter Portia, dressed like a Doctor of Laws.*]

Duke. Give me your hand. Came you from old Bellario?

Por. I did, my lord.

Duke.   You are welcome: take your place.
Are you acquainted with the difference
That holds this present question in the court?

Por. I am informèd throughly of the cause.—
Which is the merchant here, and which the Jew?

Duke. Antonio and old Shylock, both stand forth.

Por. Is your name Shylock?

Shy.   Shylock is my name.

Por. Of a strange nature is the suit you follow;
Yet in such rule that the Venetian law
Cannot impugn you as you do proceed.—
You stand within his danger, do you not?

                                [*To Antonio.*]

Ant. Ay, so he says.

Por.   Do you confess the bond?

Ant. I do.

Por.   Then must the Jew be merciful.

Shy. On what compulsion must I? Tell me that.

Por. The quality of mercy is not strained,—
It droppeth as the gentle rain from heaven
Upon the place beneath: it is twice blest;
It blesseth him that gives and him that takes:
'Tis mightiest in the mightiest: it becomes
The thronèd monarch better than his crown;
His sceptre shows the force of temporal power,
The attribute to awe and majesty,

Wherein doth sit the dread and fear of kings:
But mercy is above this sceptred sway;
It is enthronèd in the heart of kings,
It is an attribute to God himself;
And earthly power doth then show likest God's
When mercy seasons justice.—Therefore, Jew,
Though justice be thy plea, consider this,—
That, in the course of justice, none of us
Should see salvation: we do pray for mercy;
And that same prayer doth teach us all to render
The deeds of mercy. I have spoke thus much
To mitigate the justice of thy plea;
Which if thou follow, this strict court of Venice
Must needs give sentence 'gainst the merchant there.

Shy. My deeds upon my head! I crave the law,
The penalty and forfeit of my bond.

Por. Is he not able to discharge the money?

Bass. Yes, here I tender it for him in the court;
Yea, twice the sum: if that will not suffice,
I will be bound to pay it ten times o'er,
On forfeit of my hands, my head, my heart:
If this will not suffice, it must appear
That malice bears down, truth. And I beseech you.
Wrest once the law to your authority:
To do a great right, do a little wrong,
And curb this cruel devil of his will.

Por. It must not be: there is no power in Venice
Can alter a decree establishèd.

Shy. A Daniel come to judgment! yea, a Daniel!
O wise young judge, how I do honour thee!

Por. I pray you, let me look upon the bond.

Shy. Here 'tis, most reverend doctor, here it is.

*Por. Shy*lock, there's thrice thy money offered thee.

Shy. An oath, an oath, I have an oath in heaven:
Shall I lay perjury upon my soul?
No, not for Venice.

Por.   Why, this bond is forfeit;
And lawfully by this the Jew may claim
A pound of flesh, to be by him cut off
Nearest the merchant's heart.—Be merciful:
Take thrice thy money; bid me tear the bond.

Shy. When it is paid according to the tenour.—
It doth appear you are a worthy judge;
You know the law, your exposition
Hath been most sound: I charge you by the law.
Whereof you are a well-deserving pillar,
Proceed to judgment: by my soul I swear
There is no power in the tongue of man
To alter me: I stay here on my bond.

Ant. Most heartily I do beseech the court
To give the judgment.

Por.   Why, then, thus it is:—
You must prepare your bosom for his knife.

Shy. O noble judge! O excellent young man!

Por. For the intent and purpose of the law
Hath full relation to the penalty,
Which here appeareth due upon the bond.

Shy. 'Tis very true: O wise and upright judge!
How much more elder art thou than thy looks!

Por. Therefore, lay bare your bosom.

Shy.   Ay, his breast:—
So says the bond: doth it not, noble judge?
"Nearest his heart": those are the very words.

Por. It is so. Are there balance here to weigh
The flesh?

Shy.   I have them ready.

Por. Have by some surgeon, Shylock, on your charge
To stop his wounds, lest he do bleed to death.

Shy. Is it so nominated in the bond?

Por. It is not so expressed: but what of that!
'Twere good you do so much for charity.

Shy. I cannot find it; 'tis not in the bond.

Por. You, merchant, have you anything to say?

Ant. But little; I am armed and well prepared.—
Give me your hand, Bassanio; fare you well! . . .
Repent but you that you shall lose your friend,
And he repents not that he pays your debt;
For if the Jew do cut but deep enough,
I'll pay it instantly with all my heart.

Bass. Antonio, I am married to a wife
Which is as dear to me as life itself;
But life itself, my wife, and all the world,
Are not with me esteemed above thy life:
I would lose all, ay, sacrifice them all
Here to this devil, to deliver you. . . .

Shy. We trifle time: I pray thee, pursue sentence.

Por. A pound of that same merchant's flesh is thine:
The court awards it, and the law doth give it.

Shy. Most rightful judge!

Por. And you must cut this flesh from off his breast;
The law allows it, and the court awards it.

Shy. Most learnèd judge! A sentence! Come, prepare.

Por. Tarry a little; there is something else.
This bond doth give thee here no jot of blood;
The words expressly are "a pound of flesh":
Take then thy bond, take thou thy pound of flesh;
But, in the cutting it, if thou dost shed
One drop of Christian blood, thy lands and goods

Are, by the laws of Venice, confiscate
Unto the state of Venice. . . .

   Shy. Is that the law?

   Por.   Thyself shalt see the act;
For, as thou urgest justice, be assured
Thou shalt have justice, more than thou desirest. . .

   Shy. I take this offer, then; pay the bond thrice,
And let the Christian go.

   Bass.   Here is the money.

   Por. Soft!
The Jew shall have all justice; soft! no haste:
He shall have nothing but the penalty. . . .
Therefore prepare thee to cut off the flesh.
Shed thou no blood, nor cut thou less nor more
But just a pound of flesh: if thou cut'st more
Or less than a just pound,—be it but so much
As makes it light or heavy in the substance,
Or the division of the twentieth part
Of one poor scruple, nay, if the scale do turn
But in the estimation of a hair,—
Thou diest, and all thy goods are confiscate. . . .
Why doth the Jew pause? take thy forfeiture.

   Shy. Give me my principal, and let me go.

   Bass. I have it ready for thee; here it is.

   Por. He hath refused it in the open court:
He shall have merely justice, and his bond.

   Shy. Shall I not have barely my principal?

   Por. Thou shalt have nothing but the forfeiture.
To be so taken at thy peril, Jew.

   Notes:

acquaint, *v.* (acquaintance, *n.*)	= to make to know.
confiscate	= confiscated, taken as a penalty.
forfeit	= forfeited, confiscated.
impugn	= to oppose.

perjury	= false swearing.
scruple	= a small weight.
suit	= an action in a court; lawsuit.
temporal	= lasting only for a time.
tenour	= general meaning.
throughly	= thoroughly.
droppeth	= drops.
appeareth	= appears.
balance	= balances.

EXERCISES

1. Learn the speech made by Portia commencing:
   "The quality of mercy is not strained."
   This is a well-known passage in English Literature. Do not confuse *mercy* with mere *kindness*. Shylock is to show *mercy* in sparing Antonio, because he has a legal right to the pound of flesh. Note the opposition of *justice* and *mercy*: no mercy is rendered to Shylock, only justice—treatment strictly according to the law.

2. Answer these questions:
   (*a*) How was Portia dressed when she came to the court?
   (*b*) What did she go there for?
   (*c*) Who were the chief characters in the play?
   (*d*) What was Shylock's reply to Portia's plea for mercy?
   (*e*) What was Bassanio's offer? Did the Jew accept it?
   (*f*) Was Antonio prepared to pay the penalty?
   (*g*) Why did Portia ask the Jew whether there was a surgeon in attendance?
   (*h*) Did Shylock cut the flesh?
   (*i*) Did Portia allow him to take the money?
   (*j*) What did Shylock forfeit by the laws of Venice?

3. Select twelve lines in different parts of the extract. *Scan* them as you did in Exercise 3 on page 218.

4. Which of these words can be used to describe Shylock, and which Portia: cowardly, wily, brave, resourceful, cruel, cunning, timid, daring, thoughtful, clever, modest, boastful, trustful, skilful, faithful. Which words could describe any of the other characters?

AN ANGEL WITH A LUTE. (*Giovanni Bellini*)

LESSON 41

PICTURE LESSONS—VIII

The Angel with a Lute

The picture on the preceding page was painted by Giovanni Bellini, a great Italian artist who died in 1516.

In reading what has been said about the "composition" of pictures, you will have seen what care the artist takes to combine the various parts by means of connecting lines. But this is only one of many things which he must consider. He must use colours that go well together, that harmonize; and there must be a balance between the dark and light parts of his picture if he would make a fine "pattern" of it—that is to say, a thing beautiful in itself.

The "Angel with a Lute" is only part of a large picture, so you cannot see how it fits in with other parts to make a perfect whole. But it may be useful to point out, with this as an example, what a variety of light and dark (to say nothing about the variety of colours) you may expect to find in every picture that has become famous.

If you look at this "angel" carefully, you will see that certain parts appear much lighter than others, according to the colours selected by the artist; and if we were to have a photograph of it in black and white only, we should find that there are more differences in light and shade than we might have expected. Look at the picture with your eyes nearly closed and you will appreciate these differences easily.

There are the bright lights on the angel's robe, brighter than the colour of the lute, and this, again, lighter than the face and hands; and so on till we come to the dark blue above and the dark brown on the right.

Now this great variety of light and dark is one of the most important things in a picture. Generally, you will find two *broad* masses such as in the picture of "The Wood-Sawyers," where the light on one of the sawyers, and on the tree trunk, and on the grass, stands out strongly against the shadow that lies over the other parts of the picture. So in the "Salisbury Cathedral"; the building and the meadow in front of it make up a broad mass of light against the trees and the foreground.

In other words, the artist has not only to make a composition in lines and masses, but he has also to balance a mass of light against a mass of darker parts in his picture. Sometimes a very small light patch will balance a large mass of dark; and sometimes a dark spot will be sufficient against a field of light, as you may see in "The Fighting *Téméraire*," where the floating buoy in the foreground goes well with all the other bright lights and brilliant colours of the painting.

.   .   .   .   .   .

When making drawings yourself, you should try to put into practice some of the principles you have learned from this study of the great masterpieces of Art, and then some day you may perhaps be a celebrated West Indian artist.

LESSON 42

DESCRIPTIVE EXTRACTS—III

A Military Engineer in the Bahamas

Introduction.—The *Memoirs* of Peter Henry Bruce, from which the following selection is taken, were issued in 1755, and although not laying claim to high literary rank, they nevertheless show in his descriptions of Nature's gifts to the Bahamas what a keen observer was this soldier of fortune. The author went out to the Bahamas in the time of Governor Tinker, to supervise the construction of forts Nassau and Montagu. In reading this extract it must be remembered that it refers to the Bahamas as they were nearly two hundred years ago.

To convey some idea of the value of those islands, I shall endeavour to give the following account of them from my certain knowledge.

The Bahama islands enjoy the most serene and the most temperate air in all America, the heat of the sun being greatly allayed by refreshing breezes from the east; and the earth and air are cooled by constant dews which fall in the night, and by gentle showers which fall in their proper seasons; so that, as they are free from the sultry heats of our other settlements, they are as little affected with frost, snow, hail, or the north-west winds, which prove so fatal both to men and plants in our other colonies; it is therefore no wonder the sick and afflicted inhabitants of those climates fly hither for relief, being sure to find a cure here. The same causes which conduce so much to the health of man, contribute greatly to the quick growth of plants and vegetables; which here is surprising for the seeds of limes flung carelessly into the ground without any culture become, in two or three years, shrubs or little trees in full bearing.

All these islands are covered over with wood, as indeed is all America, but with this essential difference, that here the trees themselves sufficiently pay the labour of cutting them down, exclusive of the benefit which results from clearing a fertile soil; for not to mention the mastich tree, and other timber so useful in building houses, mills, etc., here are Madeira, mahogany, and cedar, all used in shipbuilding; besides vast quantities of curious woods, as prince-wood, yellow-wood, box, naked-wood (most beautifully veined and marbled), lignum vitæ, black and red iron-wood, ebony, manchineel, black feney, dog-wood, pines, palmettos, and many dyeing woods, as log-wood, brazilletta, green and yellow fustic.

They have tamarinds equal to any in the world; the Lucca olive, as well as the wild kind; oranges, lemons, limes, citrons, pomegranates, plums, sugar apples, pineapples, figs, bananas, water and musk melons, yams, gourds, cucumbers, cod and bird pepper, guavas, cassava, plantains, prickly pears, oil of castor, sugar, ginger, coffee, indigo, cotton preferable to that in the Levant, and tobacco; Indian wheat, Guinea-corn, and peas; besides these all the roots of Europe grow wonderfully quick, and to a surprising size. The flowering shrubs and other plants are so aromatic, that they perfume the air to a great distance.

The sea hereabouts abounds with fish unknown to us in Europe; those of prey are crocodiles, alligators, sharks, dolphins, sword-fish, sea-devils, spermaceti whales, grampuses, porpoises, seals, nurses, and snappers; those for food are, the king-fish, jew-fish, hog-fish, pork-fish, mutton-fish, rock-fish, Margaret-fish, coney-fish, angle-fish, bill-fish, hound-fish, gar-fish, parrot-fish, blue-fish, sucking-fish, tang-fish, trumpet-fish, porjes, groupers, jacks, hynes, old wives, grunts, skate, schoolmaster, breams, ten-pounders, stingers, ryspree, mullets, senets, barracouta, shipjacks, albe-cores, rainbow, threshers, mackerel, pilots, shads, pilchards, sailor's choice, and cavali.

Many of these are excellent eating, but such as feed on the copperas banks are poisonous, affecting the joints of those who eat them with itching pains, and the dis-order goes off by rubbing the parts; the method used to distinguish the fish is by putting a spoon, or piece of silver, into the water in which it is boiled, which turns black if the fish is poisonous.

There are no animals which can be said to be peculiar to those islands, excepting the iguana, which is found in great numbers on Andros, which lies five leagues south-west from Providence; it is a small creature, with short legs, and a short tapering tail, somewhat resembling the lizard or alligator, and is about two feet in length. On some of the other islands are numbers of wild hogs, sheep, and goats, which are produced from a breed left there by the inhabitants, and from which they are now supplied with fresh meat when they go to cut dyewoods, or rake salt at Exuma, of which they export yearly many shiploads to our northern colonies[*] on the continent.

[*] This refers to the New England States and other settlements of the English prior to American independence.

The greatest inconvenience they have here is from the plague of numerous vermin, or insects, which torment them both night and day; as bugs, cockroaches, mosquitoes, flies, sand-flies, ants, and jiggers: the last kind are no larger than a mite, and are very troublesome to strangers; they get through the soles of people's feet, and lodge between the skin and the flesh, where they lay their eggs and breed, if not timely prevented, which is done by picking them out with the point of a needle, at which the negroes are very dexterous. The ants are also very troublesome, by creeping into the houses and beds, and require care and attention to keep them from the victuals, especially sugar, of which they will carry off a great quantity in a night's time.

The mosquitoes and sand-flies come in great swarms in the evening from the woods, and the people are obliged to drive them off with smoke round their houses all night long: this inconvenience is chiefly occasioned by their not clearing the ground from those thickets of underwood; an instance of which we experienced at Fort Montagu, where I cleared away all the wood within cannon shot, and there, by that means, was happily delivered from the insects by day and night. The governor took the example, and cleared to a considerable distance from his own house, and several of the inhabitants were beginning to do the same.

PETER HENRY BRUCE.

EXERCISES

1. If you live in the Bahamas, say in what ways this description would not hold good at the present time. If you live in another country, say what differences you would expect to find if you were to visit those islands.

2. In this extract there are lists of fruits and vegetables, fishes, animals, trees, and insects. Arrange them in two groups: (i) those with which you are familiar in your own country, and (ii) those which are strange to you.

3. How did Captain Bruce keep mosquitoes and sand-flies away from his fort? What ways do you know of to do the same thing?

4. Have you been stung by a sea-egg or seaweed, or bad a jigger in your toe? If so, say what it was like.

5. Make sentences of your own containing these phrases:

convey some idea	fly hither for relief
with this essential difference	exclusive of the benefit
a surprising size	the greatest inconvenience
peculiar to those islands	is chiefly occasioned

6. Make a list of the ten words (other than nouns) you find most difficult to spell in this lesson.

7. Express in other words the meaning of each of the following:

serene	disorder
allayed	tapering
culture	dexterous
aromatic	victuals

8. Arrange these extracts in the order in which they were written:

    Jamaica (Froude).
    Port of Spain (Kingsley).
    Barbados (Froude).
    A Military Engineer in the Bahamas (Captain Bruce).

LESSON 43

THE STORY OF THE COMMONWEALTH CARIBBEAN

IN the historical lessons in this and the previous books, you have read of many interesting events which have happened in days gone by, and of the reasons why the different European nations fought so fiercely for the possession of the lands in our part of the world. We will now briefly review the story of the Commonwealth West Indies from the time of their discovery to the present day. You will then be able to learn and to understand more easily the story of your own particular colony.

With the exception of Barbados, all the West Indian islands of consequence owe their discovery to the great Genoese navigator, Christopher Columbus, who, between the years 1492 and 1504, took possession of these new lands in the name of Spain. By the papal bulls of 1493 and 1494 all the discoveries to the west of the Azores, with the exception of Brazil, were bestowed on Spain, and in 1580, when Spain annexed Portugal and her possessions, Brazil also passed into her hands, so that she then had a monopoly of the New World and its trade.

The fame of the vast wealth which was being poured into the coffers of Spain from the New World excited the enterprise of the mariners of England, and we have seen how these "gentlemen adventurers" harassed the Spanish vessels and the Spanish settlements here during the sixteenth century. The fabled El Dorado also attracted the English;

and the friendly relations which Raleigh established with the aborigines on his visits to the mainland, up the Orinoco in search of this "City of Gold," were of great service to the English, when, later on, they sought to found colonies in Guiana, although their early efforts did not meet with success.

It was during this period, too, that the want of labour in the West Indies became acute. Captain John Hawkins, a Devonshire seaman, made voyages to the coast of Guinea in 1562, where he freighted his ship with Africans, then carried them to the island of Haiti (Hispaniola), and sold them into slavery to the Spanish colonists, thus beginning the English trade in African slaves. The trade had, however, been carried on by the Spaniards and Portuguese from as early as 1503. The people of those days thought no wrong of this unholy traffic.

Towards the close of the eighteenth century, however, public opinion fortunately began to undergo a change on the subject of this trade, and the result was that on August 1, 1834, all slaves in British colonies became free.

To return to the story of the West Indies, it has been well said that their history has been written with the sword's point. Many of them changed hands several times during the seventeenth and eighteenth centuries as a result of fighting, and of all the important British islands, Barbados alone had been in the undisputed possession of England from the time of its settlement. Pride of place as the "Mother Colony of the West Indies" was held, though, by St. Kitts, as in the year 1623 Captain Thomas Warner founded there the first colony of either the English or

French dominions in the Caribbean Sea, for he "thought it would be a very convenient place for ye planting of tobaccoes, which then was a rich commoditie."

Columbus found the islands inhabited by two distinct races of Indians, the Arawaks, who lived in the "Greater Antilles" or larger islands to the north, and the Caribs, who occupied the "Lesser Antilles" or smaller islands to the east. The Arawaks proved to be a gentle and peace-loving race, and were soon crushed out of existence by the Spaniards, who compelled them to work in the mines of San Domingo. The Caribs, on the other hand, were exceedingly truculent and warlike. For many years they harassed the settlers, and it was not until 1796 that they were finally suppressed by Sir Ralph Abercromby in St. Vincent, where they had allied themselves with the French. At the present time only a few Carib families now survive in Dominica and St. Vincent. In the former island a special reserve has been set apart for their use.

Among the early settlements made by the English were those in St. Kitts (1623), Barbados (1626), Nevis (1628), Antigua (1632), Montserrat (1632), and the Bahamas (1670), while, as we read in Book IV., Jamaica was wrested from Spain in 1655.

The subsequent history of Barbados is not, like practically all the other islands, a record of warring nations, but of different factions of Englishmen striving among themselves for the mastery. Nevertheless, there have been occasions when invasion appeared to be imminent, as in 1665, when the Dutch Admiral de Ruyter arrived in

Carlisle Bay with a strong fleet, intending to reduce the island; but after a fruitless attempt at landing he withdrew.

In the eighteenth century also, during our wars with France and the American War of Independence, Barbados was in constant danger of attack until Rodney once more gave the British the command of the Caribbean by his brilliant victory in 1782. Twenty years later Barbadians were again on the defensive, when the news reached them that Villeneuve and the combined fleets of France and Spain had been sighted off St. Lucia; but the arrival of the *Victory* with Nelson on board soon allayed all fears. In the Great War, too, the safety of Barbados was once more in peril, by the presence in West Indian waters of the elusive German cruisers. The *Karlsruhe* was making for the island when she was wrecked by an internal explosion whilst only 300 miles away.

In contrast to this, St. Kitts, Nevis, Antigua, and Montserrat have had a very chequered career throughout the many struggles which have taken place there, first with the Caribs, and later with the Spanish and French. From time to time they have suffered from invasions and have changed ownership frequently, while of hurricanes and earthquakes they have had their share. The right to the possession of Dominica was long in dispute between France and Great Britain, until in 1748 the island was declared to belong to the Caribs, and to be "neutral" between the two European Powers. Then, from 1756 to 1805, there was again fighting for it at intervals, until in the end it was retained under the British flag.

Jamaica, captured during the time of the Common-wealth in England, was not highly valued by Cromwell at first, but the more the Spaniards showed a disposition to retake it, the more active he was in taking steps to retain and colonize it. Disease and want of food played havoc among the early settlers, but with the advent of Colonel Edward D'Oyley as Governor, mutiny and disorder were suppressed and the Spanish invaders from Cuba were dealt a smashing blow, thus clearing the island for English colonization.

At first it was thought that when the monarchy was restored in England, and Charles II. became king, he would give the island back to Spain, but the "Merrie Monarch" determined to retain and foster it. In 1670 it was finally ceded to England, and we have seen in other lessons how the privateers or buccaneers brought prosperity to its shores. But, while the colony prospered mightily, it had its trials and troubles; from time to time there were insurrections among the slaves, and risings of the maroons, or runaway slaves, and their descendants, who had established themselves in mountain strongholds. Violent hurricanes and appalling earthquakes have also played their part in retarding the development of the colony, as we learned in Lesson 3.

Although the Bahamas were the first part of the New World discovered by Columbus, the Spaniards did not occupy them, but carried away the natives to work in the mines or dive for pearls. It was not until the seventeenth century that these islands were frequented by vessels from Bermuda for the purpose of gathering salt. In 1670 a settlement was made by colonists from the New England States of North America, who obtained a grant of the islands from Charles II. After being plundered by the Spaniards and the French, the settlement was deserted and the islands became a nest for pirates. New Providence, where the capital, Nassau, now stands, was resettled in 1718, but was taken in turn by the American revolutionaries, by Spain, and again by Britain, in whose hands the Bahamas have remained since.

The Windward Islands of Grenada, St. Vincent, and St. Lucia were at one time inhabited by Caribs with St. Vincent as their stronghold. They were the scene of a long-continued and fierce struggle between the French and British for their possession, and in St. Lucia and Grenada particularly the French occupation has left its mark upon the religion and the language of the people. Grenada was first colonized by the French in 1650, after an unsuccessful attempt by the English in 1609, but it surrendered to a British force in 1762. In 1779 it was retaken by the French, and finally restored to Britain in 1783. The French and English agreed that, like Dominica, St. Vincent should remain a "no man's land" in possession of the Caribs, but they both nevertheless kept nibbling at it until it was eventually captured by the British in 1762. The possession of St. Lucia was a constant source of dispute between the two European nations for many years, and the struggle ended only on the 22nd of June 1803, when Morne Fortuné was carried by storm, and the island was surrendered unconditionally to Commodore Sir Samuel Hood.

Trinidad and Tobago were united into one colony from the 1st of January 1889, but previous to that date they were independent of each other. For many years after its discovery the Spaniards were unable to found a settlement in Trinidad owing to the opposition of the natives, but in 1587 a great battle was fought between the various sections of the Indians themselves, with the result that they were so weakened that it was then an easy matter for the Spaniards to gain a foothold. The English and the Dutch attacked the Spanish settlement at intervals, and, as you know, Sir Walter Raleigh spent some weeks in the island.

Trinidad does not appear to have prospered under Spanish rule, and in 1783 it was thrown open to settlers from all countries, on the condition that they were Roman Catholics, Numbers of persons therefore resorted to the colony, and during the French Revolution many French families, driven from San Domingo, Martinique, and Guadeloupe, took refuge there, making the island a French rather than a Spanish colony, but under Spanish rule. Thus the names of places are often Spanish, while the names of fishes, birds, and trees are often French. In 1797 Trinidad surrendered to a British force under Sir Ralph Abercromby and Admiral Harvey. (See Lesson 38, Book III.)

Tobago has had a very varied and turbulent history. It has changed hands more often than any other West Indian island, and has belonged in turn to Barbadians, Courlanders, privateers from Jamaica, Zeelanders, Dutch, French, and English, and we have only been in undisputed possession of it since 1814. On the headlands around its shores there are numerous dismantled cannon and other signs, such as forts and battery sites, which bear evidence to the value set upon the possession of Tobago in the old days, standing as it does like a sentinel looking out to the Atlantic.

The two British colonies on the mainland of America in the region of the West Indies must also come within the review of our story. Belize began as a settlement on the river Belize, made by retired buccaneers, under Wallis, who in 1640 was driven by the French out of Tortuga, of which he had been elected governor by his English comrades. The settlers cut the valuable timbers which they found growing in their new home and traded with the North American colonies and with the Dutch of Curacao but for a number of years they were subjected to attacks by the Spaniards, who attempted to destroy their settlement. In 1798, however, the colonists inflicted a decisive defeat upon a powerful Spanish force from Yucatan, and from that date until 1981, British Honduras (now known as Belize) remained under the British flag.

The country known until 1966 as British Guiana, which consists of Demerara, Essequibo, and Berbice, had been several times in the temporary possession of Great Britain before it was finally ceded by Holland in 1814. Columbus sighted its coast on his third voyage in 1498, and Amerigo Vespucci, to whom the continent owes its name, sailed along its shores in the following year, but owing to the hostility of the Indians the Spaniards did not settle there. We have seen that Sir Walter Raleigh explored part of it, and that the early English attempts at settlement proved failures.

The Dutch were the first to form a colony, but they made little progress until the middle of the eighteenth century, when Demerara and Essequibo were thrown open to colonists from all nations. Many persons then came from the Commonwealth West Indies and established plantations on the banks of the rivers. After changing hands from Dutch to English, then French, English, and Dutch again in turn, it finally became British in 1814. The Dutch left behind them many evidences of their occupation, such as the system of government, sea-defences for the low-lying coast-lands, and many picturesque names.

After the abolition of slavery the question of labour supply became an important one here as it did in Trinidad and other West Indies, and for many years the colony was wholly dependent on immigration from India for the increase of its agricultural population. Although immigration has ceased, East Indians now form about 50 per cent. of the total population, while in Trinidad they constitute one-third of the people of the country. You have read in previous lessons on East Indians in the West Indies of how the race has prospered in its new home.

EXERCISE

Complete the following table, showing how and when each island first came into British possession:

Colony.	Year.	How Obtained.
St. Kitts	1623	Settlement
Barbados.	. . . . . .	. . . .
Nevis.	. . . . . .	. . . .
Antigua	. . . . . .	. . . .
Montserrat. . . .	. . . . . .	. . . .
Jamaica	. . . . . .	. . . .
The Bahamas. . .	. . . . . .	. . . .
Dominica	. . . . . .	. . . .
Grenada	. . . . . .	. . . .
St. Lucia	. . . . . .	. . . .
St. Vincent	. . . . . .	. . . .
Trinidad	. . . . . .	. . . .
Tobago.	. . . . . .	. . . .
Belize.	. . . . . .	. . . .
Guyana	. . . . . .	. . . .

READING TESTS AND EXERCISES

Note.—Teachers should compile tests on the contents of this book similar to those given in the previous books. Exercises of other types are given below.

TEST I

Make a list of forty-four words from this book which you find difficult to spell. Select the most difficult word from each lesson.

TEST II

What dates are mentioned in this book? Arrange them in order of time, and indicate after each what event of importance occurred in that year.

TEST III

Make a list of the names of plants mentioned in this book. Mention some point of interest about each one.

TEST IV

(*a*) Which story in this book pleases you most. Say why.

(*b*) Which poetical selection (including those in the "Additional Poetry") do you prefer? Give reasons for your choice.

(*c*) Which quotation appeals to you most? (see pages 291–293). Why do you wish to remember it?

(*d*) Which historical incident do you consider the most interesting? Why?

TEST V

Who used the following words?

(1) "I am monarch of all I survey."

(2) "I shall never cease to regret the accident."

(3) "If another shot should take me off, behave like brave men"

(4) "I take my toll of the hard-won coal
    For my greedy furnace high."

(5) "Fair eyes look upon your deeds!"

(6) "I am out of favour with fortune."
(7) "I crave the law!"
(8) "Are you more stubborn hard than hammered iron?"
(9) "The fate of the Empire is in your hands."
(10) "Such waste was never seen."
    Find these words in this book.

TEST VI

In this test wherever a number appears there is one word, and only one word, missing. Write each word opposite to its proper number.

(a) The West Indies

The West Indies have been aptly (1) the "(2) of Sunshine." They lie within the (3), north of the (4), and there is scarcely a (5) on which the sun does not (6) upon them. Their (7) is equable and healthy, and in the months from (8) to (9), when the heat is tempered by the refreshing north-east (10) wind, it is particularly enjoyable. The scenery in the (11) is incomparably grand, and the industries (12) and varied. The (13) (14) are also rich in historical associations and traditions, and their (15) glows with the brave (16) of our gallant sailors and (17).

(b) The Approach to Jamaica

I went on deck and beheld the towering (1) mountain peak (2) high above the horizon, even at the (3) of fifty miles, with its outline clear and (4) against the splendid western (5) now gloriously (6) by the light of the set sun. We stood on under easy sail for the night, and next (7) when the (8) broke, we were off the east end of the magnificent (9) of Jamaica. The stupendous peak now (10) to rise close aboard of us, with a large solitary (11) sparkling on his forehead, and reared his forest-crowned (12) high into the cold blue (13), while the long dark (14) of the Blue Mountains, with their outlines hard and (15) in the grey light, sloped away on (16) side of him as if they had been the giant's shoulders. Great masses of (17) mist hung on their sides about half-(18) down, but all the valleys and coast as yet slept in the darkness.

HOPE. (*G. F. Watts, R.A.*)

TEST VII

A Picture Test

Hope

This beautiful picture by Watts shows Hope sitting above the world, her thoughts carried beyond it to the skies above. But she has been blindfolded, and cannot see the stars. For all that, she sings and plays on her harp though all the strings but one have snapped, leaving the instrument almost mute. This one string is slack. Hardly a sound comes from it, but Hope bends down to catch the faintest whisper. For Hope is like that—not despairing, even to the last.

What is the predominant colour in the picture? This colour stood for Heaven and Hope in old art.

To which part of the picture does the artist wish to attract our attention? What is this point known as in a picture? How does the artist succeed in drawing our gaze to this spot? (Consider the colours and leading lines as you have been shown in the earlier lessons in this book.)

Where can you find light or bright colours among the dark? Where are there straight lines among the curved? These help to make the picture more vivid, and add emphasis or force by their contrasts. Look at the other pictures by great artists in this book and see where their creators have utilized bright colours or straight lines for the same purpose.

There are two companion pictures to this one, the group forming "The Three Divine Virtues." What are the other "Virtues"? Explain how "Hope" is a fitting title for this picture.

TEST VIII

Fill in the missing words:

1. Judging by his —— he had a very weak chest.
2. The tired horses drank eagerly at the ——.
3. We gave the house a —— clean, it was so dirty.
   (In each of the above sentences the missing word ends in "ough.")

4. A swarm of ——; a shoal of ——; a hoard of ——; a battalion of ——; a caravan of ——; a litter of ——; a queue of ——. (Give the right word for each of these phrases. Teachers should add to this list.)

5. A long, low —— warned them that a snake was hid in the grass.

6. The maddened bull rushed at the man, —— him on high, and —— him to death.

7. He was so —— in his book, he did not notice how the time had flown.

8. He wrote books. He was an ——. So did his wife. She was an ——.

TEST IX

Put these words together in the right order to make them up into proverbs:

1. flock birds a
   together of feather

2. twice once
   shy bit

3. time nine in
   stitch a saves

4. stone no rolling
   a moss gathers

5. foolish wise
   penny pound

6. many there slip between
   is and a lip cup

7. ill good an wind
   that nobody it's blows

8. houses not those glass throw
   should in live stones who

QUOTATIONS WORTH REMEMBERING

THE DARKEST WATCH

The darkest watch of the night is the one before the dawn, and relief is often nearest us when we least expect it.

AUGUSTINE BIRRELLS:
From *Obiter Dicta*.

"THEY COME NOT BACK"

There are four things that come not back: the spoken word, the sped arrow, the past life, and the neglected opportunity.

From the Arabic.

TRUTH

Do not let us lie at all. Do not think of one falsehood as harmless, and another as slight, and another as unintended. Cast them all aside: it is better that our hearts should be swept clean of them, without over-care as to which is largest or blackest.

JOHN RUSKIN (1819–1900).
From *The Lamp of Truth*.

A MAN'S BEST THINGS

A man's best things are nearest him,
    Lie close about his feet;
It is the distant and the dim
    That we are sick to greet;
For flowers that grow our hands beneath
    We struggle and aspire—
Our hearts must die, except they breathe
    The air of fresh desire.

LORD HOUGHTON (1809–85).

GOOD NAME

Good name in man and woman,
Is the immediate jewel of their souls;
Who steals my purse, steals trash; 'tis something, nothing;
'Twas mine, 'tis his, and has been slave to thousands;
But he that niches from me my good name
Robs me of that which not enriches him
And makes me poor indeed.

WILLIAM SHAKESPEARE (1564–1616).
(*Othello*, Act III., Scene iii.)

THE FEAR OF DEATH

Cowards die many times before their deaths;
The valiant never taste of death but once.
Of all the wonders that I yet have heard,
It seems to me most strange that men should fear,
Seeing that death, a necessary end,
Will come, when it will come.

WILLIAM SHAKESPEARE.
(*Julius Cæsar*, Act II., Scene ii.)

A THOUGHT

Good we are and bad, and like to coins:
Some true, some light, but every one of us
Stamped with the image of the King.

LORD TENNYSON (1809–92).

NATURE

Nature is all made up of roundnesses; not the roundness of perfect globes, but of variously curved surfaces. Boughs are rounded, leaves are rounded, stones are rounded, clouds are rounded, cheeks are rounded, and curls are rounded: there is no more flatness in the natural world than there is vacancy. The world itself is round, and so is all that is in it, more or less, except human work, which is often very flat indeed.

JOHN RUSKIN.

TO PAINT THE LILY

To gild refinèd gold, to paint the lily,
To throw a perfume on the violet,
To smooth the ice, or add another hue
Unto the rainbow, or with taper light
To seek the beauteous eye of heaven to garnish
Is wasteful and ridiculous excess.

WILLIAM SHAKESPEARE.
(*King John*, Act IV., Scene i.)

REST IS NOT IDLENESS

Rest is not idleness, and to lie on the grass under the trees on a summer's day, listening to the murmur of water, or watching the clouds float across the sky, is by no means waste of time.

JOHN LUBBOCK (1834–1913).

ON BOOKS

No book is worth anything which is not worth much; nor is it serviceable, until it has been read, and re-read, and loved, and loved again; and marked, so that you can refer to the passages you want in it, as a soldier can seize the weapon he needs in an armoury, or a housewife bring the spice she needs from her store.

JOHN RUSKIN:
From *Of Kings' Treasuries*.

ADDITIONAL POETRY FOR READING AND RECITATION

THE NATIONAL ANTHEM OF ST VINCENT AND THE GRENADINES

St Vincent! Land so beautiful,
With joyful hearts we pledge to thee
Our loyalty and love, and vow
To keep you ever free.

Whate'er the future brings
Our faith will see us through,
May peace reign from shore to shore,
And God Bless and keep us true.

Hairoun! Our fair and blessed Isle,
Your mountains high, so clear and green,
Are home to me though I may stray,
A haven, calm serene.

Our little sister islands are
Those gems, the lovely Grenadines,
Upon their seas and golden sands,
The sunshine ever beams.

PHYLLIS PUNNETT.

DON CHRISTOPHER'S COVE

ST. ANN'S BAY, JAMAICA.

MILE on mile of moving blue that thunders ineffectually;
  Jet on jet of dazzling sprays that lash the shores imperiously;
Boom and hiss of broken waves whose smoke goes up perpetually,
  Moaning deep through hidden caves and whispering mysteriously.
Round the terraced limestone bluff that lifts into the rushing air
  Ranks of black pimento-bays to battle with the trade-wind's blow,
Still there walks the ghost of one that ate his heart in exile here,
  Don Cristoforo Colon, four hundred years ago.
West and East the watchful headlands question an unaltering Heaven;
  Lilac distances of mountain faint into a sail-less sea;
Out of those great emptinesses ceaselessly the sea-wind presses,
  Where Columbus heard it calling—calling as it calls to me.

SYDNEY OLIVIER.

(From "Jamaica in 1924," by permission.)

TROPIC RAIN

As the single pang of the blow, when the metal is mingled well,
Rings and lives and resounds in all the bounds of the bell,
So the thunder above spoke with a single tongue,
So in the heart of the mountain the sound of it rumbled and
    clung.
Sudden the thunder was drowned—quenched was the levin
    light—
And the angel-spirit of rain laughed out load in the night.
Loud as the maddened river raves in the cloven glen,
Angel of rain! you laughed and leaped on the roofs of men,
And the sleepers sprang in their beds, and joyed and feared as
    you fell
You struck, and my cabin quailed; the roof of it roared like a bell.
You spoke, and at once the mountain shouted and shook with
    brooks.
You ceased, and the day returned, rosy, with virgin looks.
And methought that beauty and terror are only one, not two;
And the world has room for love, and death, and thunder, and
    dew;
And all the sinews of hell slumber in summer air;
And the face of God is a rock, but the face of the rock is fair.
Beneficent streams of tears flow at the finger of pain;
And out of the cloud that smites, beneficent rivers of rain.

R. L. STEVENSON.
(*By permission of Messrs. Chatto and Windus.*)

I VOW TO THEE, MY COUNTRY

I vow to thee, my country—all earthly things above—
Entire and whole and perfect, the service of my love,
The love that asks no question; the love that stands the test,
That lays upon the altar the dearest and the best;
The love that never falters, the love that pays the price,
The love that makes undaunted the final sacrifice.
And there's another country, I've heard of long ago—
Most dear to them that love her, most great to them that know—

We may not count her armies; we may not see her King—
Her fortress is a faithful heart, her price is suffering—
And soul by soul and silently her shining bounds increase,
And her ways are ways of gentleness and all her paths are Peace.

SIR CECIL SPRING RICE.

(By permission of Lady Spring Rice.)

THE POETRY OF EARTH IS NEVER DEAD

Introduction.—Even the simplest works of Nature are beautiful, though they are not always appreciated. Poets have the gift of expressing these beauties in words, and no poet lived more constantly in an atmosphere of poetry than John Keats. He felt it everywhere, and his dearest delight was to pass on his thoughts in words for others to enjoy. To some people the chirping of grasshoppers and crickets is merely an irritating noise, but to the poet it was a form of Nature's song.

THE poetry of earth is never dead;
When all the birds are faint with the hot sun,
And hide in cooling trees, a voice will run
From hedge to hedge about the new-mown mead;
That is the grasshopper's—he takes the lead
In summer luxury; he has never done
With his delights, for when tired out with fun
He rests at ease beneath some pleasant weed.

The poetry of earth is ceasing never:
On a lone winter evening, when the frost
Has wrought a silence, from the stove there shrills
The cricket's[*] song, in warmth increasing ever,
And seems to one in drowsiness half lost
The grasshopper's among some grassy hills.

JOHN KEATS.

[*] An insect of the grasshopper order. It secretes itself in crevices near the warmth of a stove. In winter evenings the chirping noise made by the action of the wings of the male can be heard issuing from its hiding-place. Cf. *The Cricket on the Hearth*, by Charles Dickens.

THE DAY IS DONE

Introduction.—This is one of the most popular of the shorter poems written by Longfellow. Each verse contains some rare beauty of poetic thought and expression. The poet longs for quiet and peace at the end of a strenuous day, and presents to us the pure pleasures of a good man's home life. The last stanza of the poem is a favourite quotation. It is worth remembering.

THE day is done, and the darkness
    Falls from the wings of Night,
As a feather is wafted downward
    From an eagle in his flight.

I see the lights of the village
    Gleam through the rain and the mist,
And a feeling of sadness comes o'er me
    That my soul cannot resist:

A feeling of sadness and longing,
    That is not akin to pain,
And resembles sorrow only
    As the mist resembles the rain.

Come, read to me some poem,
    Some simple and heartfelt lay,
That shall soothe this restless feelings
    And banish the thoughts of day.

Not from the grand old masters,
    Not from the bards sublime,
Whose distant footsteps echo
    Through the corridors of Time.

For, like strains of martial music,
    Their mighty thoughts suggest
Life's endless toil and endeavour;
    And to-night I long for rest.

Read from some humbler poet,
    Whose songs gushed from his heart,
As showers from the clouds of summer,
    Or tears from the eyelids start;

Who, through long days of labour.
    And nights devoid of ease,
Still heard in his soul the music
    Of wonderful melodies.

Such songs have power to quiet
    The restless pulse of care,
And come like the benediction
    That follows after prayer.

Then read from the treasured volume
    The poem of thy choice,
And lend to the rhyme of the poet
    The beauty of thy voice.

And the night shall be filled with music,
    And the cares that infest the day
Shall fold their tents, like the Arabs,
    And as silently steal away.

                    H. W. LONGFELLOW.

THE BEST SCHOOL OF ALL

Introduction.—In the eyes of each one of us there is, of course, but one best school, and that is our own. No matter what others may think of theirs, our own old school is to us "the best school of all." One of our finest modern poets, Sir Henry Newbolt, celebrates in these stirring verses the memory of all our schooldays.

        IT's good to see the School we knew,
           The land of youth and dream,
        To greet again the rule we knew
           Before we took the stream:

Though long we've missed the sight of her,
　　Our hearts may not forget;
We've lost the old delight of her—
　　We keep her honour yet.

We'll honour yet the School we knew,
　　The best School of all;
We'll honour yet the rule we knew,
　　Till the last bell call.
For, working days or holidays,
And glad or melancholy days,
They were great days and jolly days
　　At the best School of all.

The stars and sounding vanities
　　That half the crowd bewitch,
What are they but inanities
　　To him that treads the pitch?
And where's the wealth, I'm wondering,
　　Could buy the cheers that roll
When the last charge goes thundering
　　Beneath the twilight goal?

The men that tanned the hide of us,
　　Our daily foes and friends,
They shall not lose their pride of us,
　　Howe'er the journey ends.
Their voice, to us who sing of it,
　　No more its message bears,
But the round world shall ring of it,
　　And all we are be theirs.

To speak of fame a venture is
　　There's little here can bide,
But we may face the centuries,
　　And dare the deepening tide;

For though the dust that's part of us
   To dust again be gone,
Yet here shall beat the heart of us—
   The School we handed on!

We'll honour yet the School we knew,
   The best School of all;
We'll honour yet the rule we knew,
   Till the last bell call.
For, working days or holidays,
And glad or melancholy days,
They were great days and jolly days
   At the best School of all.

SIR HENRY NEWBOLT.
(By permission of the Author.)

ALEXANDER SELKIRK

   Introduction.—These verses are supposed to be written by Alexander Selkirk during his solitary abode on the desert island of Juan Fernandez, in the Pacific Ocean, off the coast of South America. He was landed there by his own request in 1704, and lived alone till 1709, when he was taken off by a passing ship. His story is supposed to have given Defoe the idea of writing *Robinson Crusoe,* but the writer placed the island in the West Indies, and all West Indians know that Tobago has the reputation of being "Crusoe's Isle."

I AM monarch of all I survey,
   My right there is none to dispute;
From the centre all round to the sea,
   I am lord of the fowl and the brute.
O Solitude!* where are the charms
   That sages have seen in thy face?
Better dwell in the midst of alarms,
   Than reign in this horrible place.

I am out of humanity's † reach,
   I must finish my journey alone,
Never hear the sweet music of speech—
   I start at the sound of my own.

---

* State of being alone.   † Mankind's.

The beasts that roam over the plain
    My form with indifference * see;
They are so unacquainted with man,
    Their tameness is shocking to me.

Ye winds, that have made me your sport
    Convey to this desolate shore
Some cordial,† endearing report
    Of a land I shall visit no more.
My friends, do they now and then send
    A wish or a thought after me?
O tell me I yet have a friend,
    Though a friend I am never to see.

How fleet is the glance of the mind!
    Compared with the speed of its flight,
The tempest itself lags behind,
    And the swift-wingèd arrow of light.
When I think of my own native land,
    In a moment I seem to be there;
But, alas! recollection at hand
    Soon hurries me back to despair.

But the sea-fowl is gone to her nest,
    The beast is laid down in his lair
Even here is a season of rest,
    And I to my cabin repair.
There's mercy in every place,
    And mercy, encouraging thought!
Gives even affliction a grace,
    And reconciles man to his lot.

                    WILLIAM COWPER (1731–1800).

* Without interest or fear.   † Hearty.

THE NATIONAL ANTHEM OF ST LUCIA

Sons and daughters of St Lucia
Love the land that gave us birth
Land of beaches, hills and valleys
Fairest Isle of all the earth.
Where-so-ever you may roam
Love, oh love our island home

Gone the times when nations battled
For this 'Helen of the West'!
Gone the days when strife and discord
Dimmed her children's toil and rest.
Dawns at last a brighter day
Stretches out a glad, new way.

May the Good Lord bless our Island
Guard her sons from woe and harm!
May our people live united,
Strong in soul and strong in arm,
Justice, Truth and Charity
Our Ideal forever be.

THE NATIONAL ANTHEM OF ANTIGUA AND BARBUDA

Fair Antigua and Barbuda
We thy sons and daughters stand
Strong and firm in peace or danger
To safeguard our native land.
We commit ourselves to building
A true nation brave and free
Ever striving, ever seeking
Dwell in love and unity.

Raise the standard raise it boldly
Answer now to duty's call
To the service of your country
Sparing nothing, giving all.
Gird your loins and join the battle
'Gainst fear, hate and poverty
Each endeavouring, all achieving,
Live in peace where man is free.

God of nations, let thy blessings
Fall upon this land of ours;
Rain and sunshine never ending
Fill her fields with crops and flowers.
We her children do implore thee
Give us strength, faith, loyalthy.
Never failing, all enduring
To defend her liberty.